Jürgen Beyerer | Fernando Puente León | Thomas Längle (Eds.)

OCM 2019

4th International Conference on Optical Characterization of Materials

March 13th – 14th, 2019
Karlsruhe | Germany

OCM 2019

4th International Conference on Optical Characterization of Materials

March 13th – 14th, 2019
Karlsruhe | Germany

Edited by
Jürgen Beyerer | Fernando Puente León | Thomas Längle

KIT Scientific Publishing

Veranstalter

Fraunhofer Institut of Optronics,
System Technologies and Image Exploitation IOSB
c/o Karlsruhe Center for Material Signatures KCM
Fraunhoferstraße 1, 76131 Karlsruhe

Dieser Tagungsband ist auch als Onlineversion abrufbar unter
http://dx.doi.org/10.5445/KSP/1000087509

Impressum

KIT Scientific Publishing

Karlsruher Institut für Technologie (KIT)
KIT Scientific Publishing
Straße am Forum 2
D-76131 Karlsruhe

KIT Scientific Publishing is a registered trademark
of Karlsruhe Institute of Technology.
Reprint using the book cover is not allowed.

www.ksp.kit.edu

Print on Demand 2019 – Gedruckt auf FSC-zertifiziertem Papier

ISBN 978-3-7315-0864-9
DOI 10.5445/KSP/1000087509

Preface

The state of the art in optical characterization of materials is advancing rapidly. New insights into the theoretical foundations of this research field have been gained and exciting practical developments have taken place, both driven by novel applications and innovative sensor technologies that are constantly emerging. The big success of the international conferences on Optical Characterization of Materials in 2013, 2015 and 2017 proves the necessity of a platform to present, discuss and evaluate the latest research results in this interdisciplinary domain. Due to that fact, the international conference on Optical Characterization of Materials (OCM) took place the fourth time in March 2019.

The OCM 2019 was organized by the Karlsruhe Center for Spectral Signatures of Materials (KCM) in cooperation with the German Chapter of the Instrumentation & Measurement Society of IEEE. The Karlsruhe Center for Spectral Signatures of Materials is an association of institutes of Karlsruhe Institute of Technology (KIT) and the business unit Automated Visual Inspection of the Fraunhofer Institute of Optronics, System Technologies and Image Exploitation IOSB.

Despite the conference's young age, the organizing committee has had the pleasure to evaluate a large amount of abstracts. Based on the submissions, we selected 22 papers as talks, a keynote lecture and several practical demonstrations.

The present book is based on the conference held in Karlsruhe, Germany from March 13–14, 2019. The aim of this conference was to bring together leading researchers in the domain of Characterization of Materials by spectral characteristics from UV (240 nm) to IR (14 µm), multispectral image analysis, X-ray methods, polarimetry, and microscopy. Typical application areas for these techniques cover the fields of, e.g., food industry, recycling of waste materials, detection of contaminated materials, mining, process industry, and raw materials.

The editors would like to thank all of the authors that have contributed to these proceedings as well as the reviewers, who have invested a generous amount of their time to suggest possible improvements of the papers. The help of Henning Schulte, Jürgen Hock and Anja Shevchyk in the preparation of this book is greatly appreciated. Last but not least, we thank the organizing committee of the conference, led by Britta Ost, for their effort in organizing this event. The excellent technical facilities and the friendly staff of the Fraunhofer IOSB greatly contributed to the success of the meeting.

March 2019

Jürgen Beyerer
Fernando Puente León
Thomas Längle

General Chairs

Jürgen Beyerer	Fraunhofer IOSB Karlsruhe
Fernando Puente León	Karlsruhe Institute of Technology

Program Chair

Thomas Längle	Karlsruhe

Program Committee

Sebastian Bauer	Madison (Wisconsin)
Mark Bücking	Schmallenberg
Robin Gruna	Karlsruhe
Michael Heizmann	Karlsruhe
Thomas Hofmann	Würzburg
Olfa Kanoun	Chemnitz
Halit Z. Kuyumcu	Berlin
Johannes Meyer	Karlsruhe
Dirk Nüßler	Wachtberg
Thomas Pretz	Aachen
Matthias Richter	Karlsruhe
Félix Salazar	Madrid
Heinar Schmidt	Kulmbach
Henning Schulte	Karlsruhe
Miro Taphanel	Karlsruhe
Hermann Wotruba	Aachen
Bernhard Zagar	Linz

Contents

Algorithms

Spectral Sensors

Determination of tomato quality attributes using portable NIR-sensors

Simon Goisser[1], Julius Krause[2,3], Michael Fernandes[4], and Heike Mempel[1]

[1] University of Applied Sciences Weihenstephan Triesdorf, Greenhouse Technology and Quality Management, Am Staudengarten 10, 85354 Freising
[2] Karlsruhe Institute of Technology, Vision and Fusion Laboratory IES, Haid-und-Neu-Str. 7, 76131 Karlsruhe
[3] Fraunhofer Institute of Optronics, System Technologies and Image Exploitation IOSB, Visual Inspection Systems, Fraunhoferstr. 1, 76131 Karlsruhe
[4] Deggendorf Institute of Technology, Technology Campus Grafenau, Department of Applied Artificial Intelligence, Hauptstraße 3, 94481 Grafenau

Abstract As part of a research project a multidisciplinary approach of different research institutes is followed to investigate the possibility of using a commercially available miniaturized NIR-sensor for the determination of tomato fruit quality parameters in postharvest. Correlation of spectra and tomato reference values of firmness, dry matter and total soluble solids showed good prediction accuracy. Additionally the decline of firmness over storage time with respect to storage temperature of tomatoes could be modelled. Therefore, the decline of firmness as an indicator for shelf-life can be predicted using this portable NIR-Sensor.

Keywords: NIR, portable, tomato, brix, firmness, dry matter.

1 Introduction

At the moment, grading and sorting of fresh produce is highly dominated by external and internal quality attributes like colour, fruit texture and sugar content. Some of these requirements are statutory and written down in marketing standards for fresh fruit and vegetables [1]. In order to guarantee internal quality like sweetness and taste of produce, additional testing of internal quality parameters like sugar content or sugar-acid ratio is necessary for certain products alongside these statutory criteria standards. The determination of internal parameters is often time consuming and requires destructive measurement methods. Immediately after harvest the quality of fruits and vegetables changes due to ongoing metabolic processes. Depending on various parameters like fruit maturity, packaging and storage conditions, quality of post harvest produce decays in different time periods. Sensitive fruits like strawberries have a shelf life of only a few days, whereas more robust fruits like apples can be stored for up to nearly one year under appropriate storage conditions. Climacteric fruits like tomatoes underlie post-ripening, which on one hand can lead to longer shelf life, but on the other hand cause alteration of sensorial parameters like taste or haptic. Furthermore, firmness is an important indicator of tomato quality which determines shelf life and influences consumer's acceptance [2]. Tomato is one of the most important fruits cultivated in Germany, with a total percentage of nearly 30 % of Germany's greenhouse production area for vegetables [3] and number one vegetable with respect to per capita consumption [4]. Sugar content, acidity and the acid-brix ratio are internal quality parameters that can help to determine the ripening stage and affect the taste of tomatoes. In the past, various studies were conducted to prove that some of these parameters can be predicted using near-infrared spectroscopy (NIRS) on different tomato varieties [5, 6]. NIRS is well suited for quality control of fresh produce because it is non-destructive and requires little to no sample preparation. Additionally, NIRS techniques can be used as multidimensional predictors to determine various parameters in one work-step. Due to an ongoing technical development and miniaturization in the field of NIR spectrometers, companies are offering small and portable sensors. These devices can be used in numerous applications throughout the agro-food and horticultural industry, as illustrated by dos Santos et al. [7]. The technique of NIR is already applied in sorting and grading machines, especially for high quality produce which are ripened in post-harvest processes (e. g., mango, avocado). In contrast to bulky benchtop devices, these hand-held sensors allow a transfer of NIR techniques from the laboratory to in-field and other applications along the whole horticultural supply chain of fresh produce. In addition to the determination of specific fruit quality parameters, these devices could unlock potential in measuring the maturity or ripening stage of fresh produce with respect to remaining shelf life. A measurement tool which allows the quantification of shelf life could help to reduce the amount of annual food loss of around 11 million tons [8] in Germany. First studies indicate that there is high potential for predicting the quality of fresh fruits and vegetables with portable and miniaturized NIR devices. According to Kusumiyati et al. [9], the use of a portable NIR-device and PLSR analysis proved feasibility of predicting the on-tree firmness of tomatoes with $r^2 = 0{,}88$ and a standard error of prediction of 0,09 MPa as well as lightness value L* ($r^2 = 0.96$, SEP = 3.19) and color value a* ($r^2 = 0{,}98$, SEP = 3,13). Some startup companies focus on this development and launch various miniaturized NIR-handheld devices called food-scanners, promising end-consumers a fast and nondestructive measurement of various food traits like protein, sugar or total energy content [10]. A first study by Kaur et al. [11], which examined the performance of different portable and commercially available spectrometers with respect to the prediction of dry matter, showed promising results for a combined data set of apples, kiwifruit and summerfruit (rp^2 of 0,93-0,95). Subsequent research investigated the on-tree prediction of 'Hass' avocado harvest maturity using the F-750 spectrometer (Felix Instruments) and found suitable prediction models for dry matter ($rp^2 = 0.98$; RMSEP = 0.25 %) and oil content ($rp^2 = 0.96$; RMSEP = 1.14 %) [12]. A current study, focusing on the performance of a consumer scale SCiO (Consumer Physics) molecular sensor by Li et al. (2018), found good results for the prediction of total soluble solids in kiwifruit ($RVal^2 = 0.77$; RMSEp = 0.76 %) and potential in classifying feijoa according to maturity and 'Hass' avocado according to ripening stage, whereas the prediction of apple quality was not feasible. In summary, miniaturized NIR devices seem to hold potential in predicting the quality of fresh produce, making it a good method of choice in investigating the feasibility for quality predictions of tomato fruit. At the moment, a key challenge for a successful implementation in supply chain processes is the provision of suitable prediction models of fresh produce. Since different types of produce require specific calibrations, further work is required to investigate predictable fruit quality parameters and to build up data collections, which allow a robust calibration of portable devices. As part of the alliance "Wir retten Lebensmittel", initiated by the Bavarian Ministry of Food, Agriculture and Forestry, a multidisciplinary approach of different research institutes was conducted during a two-year research project. The aim of this work was to investigate the possibility of using a self-built and miniaturized NIR-sensor for the determination of tomato fruit maturity parameters such as sugar content, firmness and dry matter. A similar approach with focus on a commercially available pocket-sized NIR-sensor has already been performed (publication in review process). Based on these results, storage experiments were carried out in order to evaluate the feasibility of predicting shelf life of tomatoes with NIR-sensors. Tomato was chosen as model fruit because of its economic importance. An early determination of maturity as well as shelf life of tomatoes could help to control the supply chain and take alternative paths for produce not suitable for the fresh market (e. g., processing into soups, juices or smoothies). Furthermore, appropriate measures like sales promotions of ripe fruits can be launched in order to reduce food waste.

2 Material and methods

2.1 Sample material

Cherry- and salad-tomatoes (*Solanum lycopersicum* 'EZ 1359' and 'EZ 1256') from a greenhouse of the University of Applied Sciences Weihenstephan-Triesdorf (latitude 48°24′6″N and longitude 11°43′53″E) were used as sample material. Tomato plants were cultivated in a run-to-waste system on rock wool. Determination of sugar content, firmness, dry matter and color values of tomato fruits was done during the summer of 2017 at the Institute of Horticulture, Freising, Germany.

2.2 Methods and storage conditions

In a first experiments, 40 salad- and 40 cherry-tomatoes were harvested and the spectra recorded. Afterwards, sugar content in terms of TSS-concentration of each individual fruit was measured. In a second experiment, 120 tomatoes (60 cherry and 60 salad) were harvested and stored at room temperature (20 - 22 °C) for two weeks to evaluate post-ripening-processes with respect to changes in fruit skin color and dry matter. Every two days, spectra of ten fruits of each variety were taken and fresh weight, dry weight and color values of each fruit was recorded. In order to model shelf life and the decay of tomato fruit firmness over time, a third experiment was conducted using different storage conditions. 320 salad- and 360 cherry- tomatoes were harvested from the greenhouse. Spectra was recorded and firmness measured of 16 salad- and 20 cherry-tomatoes to determine initial fruit firmness. The remaining tomatoes were stored in batches of equal size under three different storage conditions at 8, 15 and 20 °C and relative humidity of 96 - 98 % respectively using laboratory refrigerators (Liebherr Mediline model LKPv 6522, Liebherr-International GmbH, Biberach, Germany). The resulting vapor pressure deficits were 2,1 - 4,3 hPa (8 °C), 3,4 - 6,8 hPa (15 °C) and 4,6 - 9,4 hPa (20°C). Every two to three days, the spectra of ten fruits of each variety and storage condition were recorded and firmness was measured. Due to moldiness and other physiological disorders during storage, 6 salad- and 11 cherry-tomatoes had to be excluded from the experiment, resulting in a valid data set of 314 salad- and 349 cherry-tomatoes.

2.3 Recording of NIR spectra

Spectroscopic measurements were performed using a self-built handheld NIR spectrometer consisting of a DLP® NIRscan™ Nano Evaluation Module (Texas Instruments, Dallas, Texas), supporting wavelengths from 900 - 1700 nm, embedded in a custom-built aluminum case (see Fig. 1A.). The method of measurement is diffuse reflection. Spectra of tomatoes were recorded by taking eight separate measurements orthogonally around the equator of each fruit (see 1.1) using a reprogrammed graphical user interface (GUI). The eight spectra for each fruit were averaged afterwards.

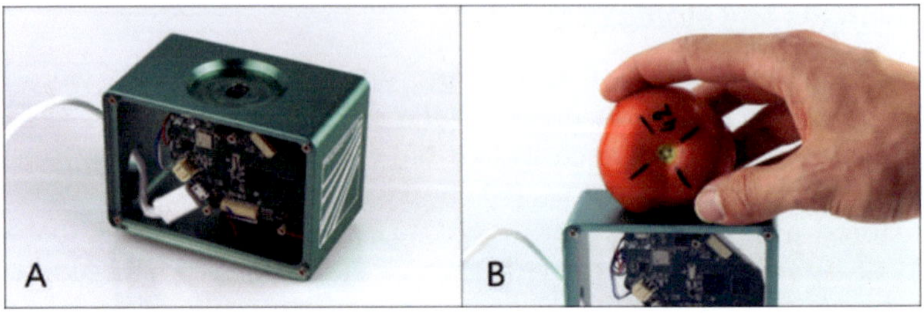

Figure 1.1: Custom-built hand held NIR spectrometer (A) and recording of tomato spectra around the fruit equator (B)

2.4 Acquisition of reference data

Reference measurements were performed immediately after recording spectra. Total soluble solids (TSS) were measured according to the OECD fruit and vegetable scheme by squeezing two longitudinal slices from opposite sides of the fruit with a garlic press and measuring the mixed juice with a digital refractometer HI 96801 (Hanna Instruments, Woonsocket, USA). The results, in degrees Brix, were recorded to one decimal place. The concentration of dry matter (DM) was measured gravimetrically for whole tomatoes. Weight of fresh fruits was determined to the nearest 0,001 g. Subsequently fruits were dried in an oven at 105 °C for 48 h. The final dry weight was determined to the nearest 0,001 g and DM calculated as the percentage of dry weight to initial fresh weight of each fruit. Firmness was measured using a non-invasive hand-held penetrometer AGROSTA 100X (Agro Technologie, Serqueux, France) specifically designed to measure tomatoes and berries. The penetrometer expresses firmness of fruits in a unit of percent in a range from 0 - 100, whereas 100 percent equals 8,09 Newton. Results were converted to Newton by taking account of penetrometer-pin-diameter and the maximum force used to push in the metal pin. Measurements were taken at two spots on opposite sides of the equator of each tomato. Both readings for each tomato were averaged. Additionally a subjective firmness bonitur was performed by the first author, grading tomatoes into the bonitur classes A (very firm), B (firm) and C (soft).

3 Results and discussion

The data analysis was performed with *Python* using the *scikit-learn* framework [13]. After a normalization in the first step, the regression models were developed to establish a relationship between the normalized spectra and the properties of salad and cherry tomatoes. To verify the models a *leave-one-out-cross-validation* (LOOCV) was performed.

3.1 Spectral preprocessing

To reduce scattering effects and noise, spectral preprocessing was applied. Because of the signal-to-noise ratio, the spectral range for the analysis was reduced to 198 bands between 901 nm and 1608 nm. For noise suppression, the mean value of all spectra of a sample was calculated and in addition, the mean value spectra were smoothed with a Savitzky-Golay filter (15,3). In a further step, the first derivative was formed to correct the baseline due to different scattering properties. Finally, different intensities were compensated by normalization using Standard Normal Variate (SNV).

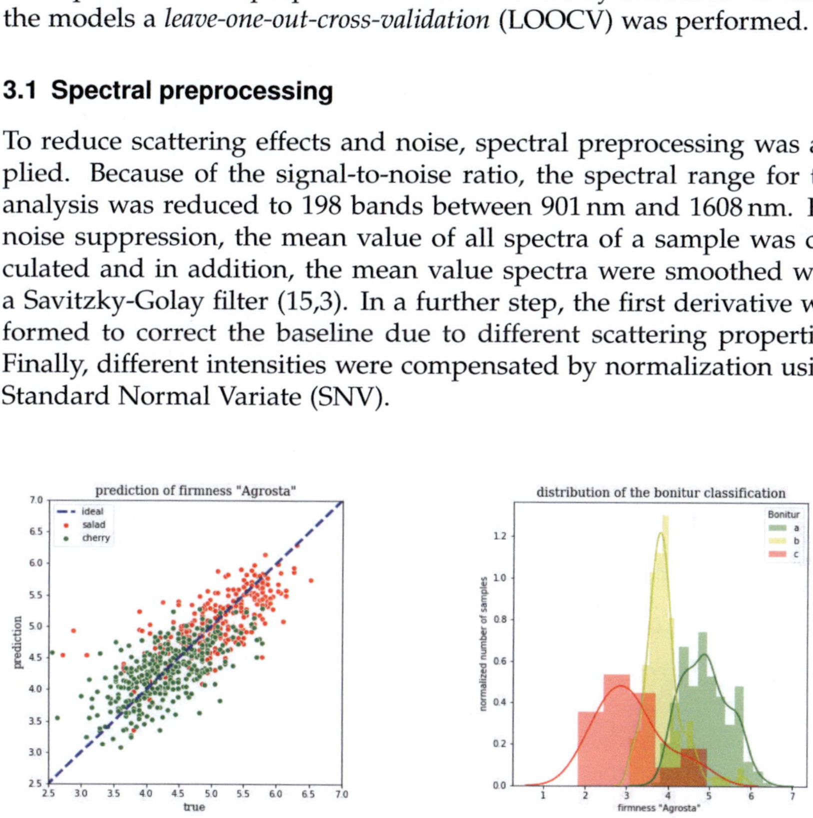

Figure 1.2: PLSR prediction of the dry matter using the normalized spectra. The multi-product model works well for both varieties. (RMESP 'salad' = 0.45, RMESP 'cocktail' =0.45). The bonitur classification is related to the firmness. Therefore, a clear dependence of the quality score on the measured firmness can be seen.

3.2 Prediction of quality attributes

The normalized spectra can be used to predict the firmness of the tomato by a partial least squares regression modell (PLSR) modell. A multi-product PLSR model was developed, which was trained with the spectra of both varieties. The root-mean-square-error-of-prediction (RMSEP) of the model determined in a cross validation is 0.52 for salad tomatoes and 0.5 for cherry tomatoes (see fig. 1.2).

There is also a relationship between the optically and mechanically measurable firmness and the quality evaluation of the bonitur (see fig. 1.2). This allows classification into three quality levels on the basis of the measurable firmness.

In addition to the firmness, which can be used as the main criterion for freshness and shelf life, further parameters were determined. First, the dry matter was evaluated. It should be noted that the correlation coefficient between strength and dry matter has a value of 0.77. In a multi-product calibration of 40 salad and 40 cherry tomatoes a PLSR model for the prediction of dry matter could be created. The RMSEP of the dry matter was 0.50 and 0.52, respectively, with the values of both varieties ranging between 5 % and 9 % dry matter.

To predict the brix value, a multi-product calibration for salad and cocktail tomatoes using PLSR was also made. The brix value of the tomatoes could be determined with an RMSEP of 0.56 and 0.68 °brix for salad and cocktail tomatoes in the range between 4 and 9 °brix .

3.3 Prediction of shelf life

In this regard, firmness can be used as one of the parameters to estimating shelf life of tomatoes. To this end, the time dependency over storage can be modeled by using the Arrhenius equations [14,15].

Data analysis is performed through the packet R software. The loss of firmness for all three-temperature levels as well as the final models for the three temperature levels are plotted in Figure 1.3. The kinetic parameters as well as the activation energy can then be extracted from the model. In Figure 1.3 the quality classes A, B and C are presented based on bonitur classifications. It shows that along the storage of tomatoes, the subjectively perceived firmness declines due to vapor pressure deficit and storage time. Since in this experiment, the vapore

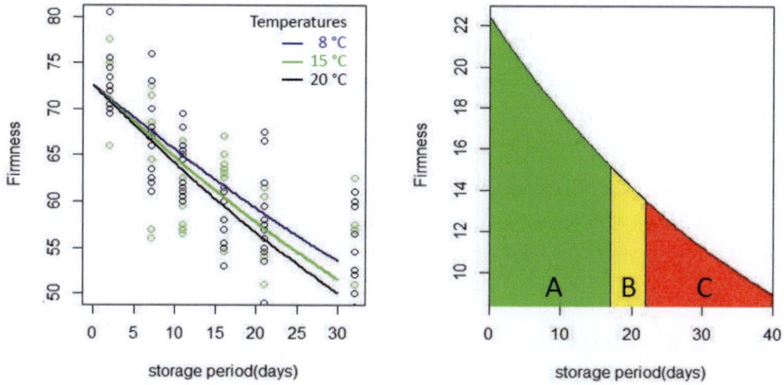

Figure 1.3: Firmness measured at 3 different temperature levels [8°,15°,20°C] and the fitted curves of the Arrhenius models (left). Firmness – storage time model for temperature 20°C indicating 3 different quality classes for salad tomatoes (right)

pressure deficit was relatively small, the influence of storage period is rated higher than the influence due to temperature. By considering the storage conditions at the point of sale with notably higher vapor pressure deficits (e. g. 50,2 hPa at 20°C and 50 % relative humidity) a faster decline in firmness can be expected.

4 Summary

Firmness is a strong parameter for quality of tomatoes. However, the measurement of firmness using classical measuring methods like penetrometers leads to fruit damage, manifesting itself in bruises and subsequently in a fast decay of the fruits. A similar practice can bee seen in supermarkets when consumers try to assess quality by touching the fruits. In both cases a non-destructive and non-contact optical measurement offers an advantage [16]. The results of this study show that firmness can be predicted with good accuracy using a miniaturized NIR-sensor. Furthermore, a relation between bonitur classifications and objective firmness measurements was established, indicating the possibility of distinguishing bonitur grades by means of NIR-spectroscopy. It is also shown that the decline of firmness over storage time with respect to vapor pressure deficit of tomatoes can be modelled. In combination, the decline of firmness as an indicator for shelf-life can be predicted using this portable NIR-Sensor.

Future work should address the validity of the PLSR correlation by adding new tomato varietes to the data set. Regarding the utilization of portable NIR-sensors by end-consumers these data sets should focus on varieties available in supermarkets.

Acknowledgement

This work was supported by the Bavarian Ministry of Food, Agriculture and Forestry as part of the alliance "Wir retten Lebensmittel".

References

1. UNECE, "Fresh fruit and vegetables - standards," 2017. [Online]. Available: https://www.unece.org/trade/agr/standard/fresh/ffv-standardse.html
2. A. Batu, "Determination of acceptable firmness and colour values of tomatoes," *Journal of Food Engineering*, vol. 61, no. 3, pp. 471–475, 2004.
3. M. Koch, "Fläche im unterglasanbau steigt weiter," 2018. [Online]. Available: https://www.ami-informiert.de/ami-maerkte/maerkte/ami-gartenbau/ami-meldungen-gartenbau/single-ansicht/singleview/news/artikel/flaeche-im-unterglasanbau-steigt-weiter.html
4. B. Rogge, "Blumenkohl mit kräftigem mengenplus in den top-10," 2018. [Online]. Available: https://www.ami-informiert.de/ami-maerkte/maerkte/ami-gartenbau/ami-meldungen-gartenbau/single-ansicht/singleview/news/artikel/blumenkohl-mit-kraeftigem-mengenplus-in-den-top-10.html
5. K. Flores, M.-T. Sánchez, D. Pérez-Marín, J.-E. Guerrero, and A. Garrido-Varo, "Feasibility in nirs instruments for predicting internal quality in intact tomato," *Journal of Food Engineering*, vol. 91, no. 2, pp. 311–318, 2009.
6. G. Kim, D.-Y. Kim, G. H. Kim, and B.-K. Cho, "Applications of discrete wavelet analysis for predicting internal quality of cherry tomatoes using vis/nir spectroscopy," *Journal of Biosystems Engineering*, vol. 38, no. 1, pp. 48–54, 2013.

7. C. A. T. dos Santos, M. Lopo, R. N. M. J. Páscoa, and J. A. Lopes, "A review on the applications of portable near-infrared spectrometers in the agro-food industry," *Applied spectroscopy*, vol. 67, no. 11, pp. 1215–1233, 2013.

8. M. Kranert, G. Hafner, J. Barabosz, H. Schuller, D. Leverenz, A. Kölbig, F. Schneider, S. Lebersorger, and S. Scherhaufer, "Ermittlung der weggeworfenen lebensmittelmengen und vorschläge zur verminderung der wegwerfrate bei lebensmitteln in deutschland," 2012.

9. Kusumiyati, T. Akinaga, M. Tanaka, and S. Kawasaki, "On-tree and after-harvesting evaluation of firmness, color and lycopene content of tomato fruit using portable nir spectroscopy," *Journal of Food, Agriculture & Environment*, vol. 6, no. 2, 2008.

10. G. Rateni, P. Dario, and F. Cavallo, "Smartphone-based food diagnostic technologies: A review," *Sensors (Basel, Switzerland)*, vol. 17, no. 6, 2017.

11. H. Kaur, R. Künnemeyer, and A. McGlone, "Comparison of hand-held near infrared spectrophotometers for fruit dry matter assessment," *Journal of Near Infrared Spectroscopy*, vol. 25, no. 4, pp. 267–277, 2017.

12. K. Ncama, L. S. Magwaza, C. A. Poblete-Echeverría, H. H. Nieuwoudt, S. Z. Tesfay, and A. Mditshwa, "On-tree indexing of 'hass' avocado fruit by non-destructive assessment of pulp dry matter and oil content," *Biosystems Engineering*, vol. 174, pp. 41–49, 2018.

13. F. Pedregosa, G. Varoquaux, A. Gramfort, V. Michel, B. Thirion, O. Grisel, M. Blondel, P. Prettenhofer, R. Weiss, V. Dubourg, J. Vanderplas, A. Passos, D. Cournapeau, M. Brucher, M. Perrot, and E. Duchesnay, "Scikit-learn: Machine learning in Python," *Journal of Machine Learning Research*, vol. 12, pp. 2825–2830, 2011.

14. J. Pinheiro, C. Alegria, M. Abreu, E. M. Gonçalves, and C. L. Silva, "Kinetics of changes in the physical quality parameters of fresh tomato fruits (Solanum lycopersicum, cv. 'Zinac') during storage," *Journal of Food Engineering*, vol. 114, no. 3, pp. 338–345, feb 2013. [Online]. Available: https://www.sciencedirect.com/science/article/abs/pii/S0260877412004074

15. C. Van Dijk, C. Boeriu, F. Peter, T. Stolle-Smits, and L. Tijskens, "The firmness of stored tomatoes (cv. Tradiro). 1. Kinetic and near infrared models to describe firmness and moisture loss," *Journal of Food Engineering*, vol. 77, no. 3, pp. 575–584, dec 2006. [Online]. Available: https://www.sciencedirect.com/science/article/abs/pii/S0260877405005224

16. M. Geyer, M. Linke, I. Gerbert, O. Schlüter, and H.-P. Kläring, "Beurteilen der Haltbarkeit klimakterischer Früchte am Beispiel der

Tomate," *LANDTECHNIK – Agricultural Engineering*, vol. 63, no. 3, pp. 158–159, jun 2008. [Online]. Available: https://www.landtechnik-online.eu/ojs-2.4.5/index.php/landtechnik/article/view/2008-3-158-159

NIR spectroscopy for cacao bean quality measurements

Claudia Beleites[1,2], Michael Glitschka[1],
Christoph Böttcher[1], and Andrea Krähmer[1]

[1] Julius Kühn-Institut
Königin-Luise-Str. 19, Berlin, Germany
[2] Chemometric Consulting and Chemometrix GmbH
both Södeler Weg 19, Wölfersheim, Germany

Abstract We present experimental design strategies for developing predictive chemometric models based on NIR spectra of plant materials (here: *Cacao* beans) with a particular focus on two issues: Identifying important confounding factors and choosing a relevant subset of samples for reference analysis.

Keywords: NIR spectroscopy, design of experiments, nested design, hierarchical/clustered data, calibration, regression.

1 Introduction

Project CocoaChain studies cacao/cocoa quality along the processing chain. Setting up an analytical method based on NIR spectroscopy and chemometric data analysis for measuring various aspects of Cacao bean quality and using these NIR spectra to actually derive conclusions about the cacao beans on the first glance have similar sample reqirements: Both need a suitable set of samples (specimen) of which NIR spectra are then measured. For the NIRS modeling, however additional reference information is needed, while for quality assessment the obtained NIRS method predicts these characteristics.

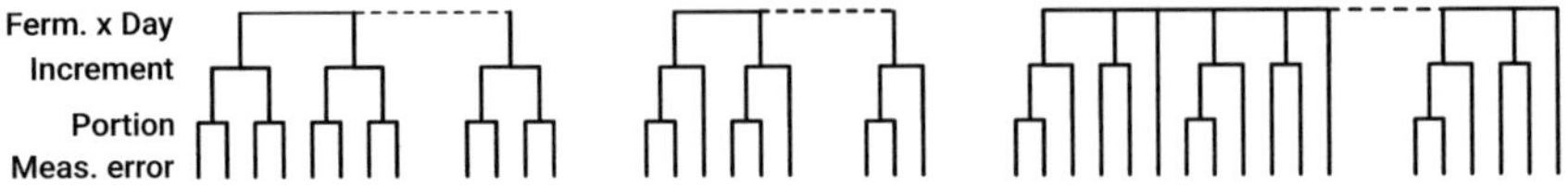

Figure 2.1: Designs of Experiments (DoE) for nested data structures.

Analytical procedures as well as biological systems and production processes often have deeply nested structures of influencing or confounding factors. Experimental effort is most efficiently spent if concentrated on the large and important confounders. At the same time, reference analyses are often expensive and/or time-consuming and in fact a bottleneck for the NIR calibration, emphasizing the need to spend the available experimental effort well.

In his seminal paper [1], Bainbridge presented three different designs of experiments (see fig. 2.1) that allow estimating contributions of nested sources of random error. The fully nested design is easiest to analyze, but it comes at the cost of the number of measurements/samples at the lowest level of the data structure exponentially growing with the number of factors (hierarchy levels) considered. In addition, the degrees of freedom are concentrated in this lowermost level of the data hierarchy, which is also the variance component that is easiest to estimate. In other words, this design is inefficient in its use of measurements for the higher variance components. In contrast, the staggered nested design leads to almost equally distributed degrees of freedom across the data hierarchy. Still, variance componence further up are more difficult to estimate, so a design such as the inverted nested design that concentrates degrees of freedom rather on the top levels would be even better. However, at the time Bainbridge wrote his paper (1965) inverted nested design data could not be analyzed. With the nowadays readily available statistical software tools such as mixed models, it is now easily possible to employ such even further thinned out designs.

In this presentation, we explore the application of these designs for analytical method development, namely NIRS calibration and the corresponding reference analyses.

Table 2.1: Overview of the fermentations sampled in Peru 2018. Samples P1 – P4 are commercially imported cacao from the same cooperative where sampling took place in Quillabamba.

Fermentation ID	Region	Variety	Days sampled
KZug	Tingo Maria	CCN51	7
1	Quillabamba	Chuncho	7
2	Quillabamba	Chuncho	6
7	Quillabamba	Chuncho	1 (end)
8	Quillabamba	Chuncho	1 (end)
3	Tarapoto	Forastero CCN51	8
4	Tarapoto	Forastero CCN51	8
9	Tarapoto	Criollo ICS 95 + other	1 (end)
10	Tarapoto	Criollo ICS 95 + other	1 (end)
13	Piura	Cacao blanco + Cacao violeta	7
P1	Quillabamba	Chuncho	n
P2	Quillabamba	Chuncho	n
P3	Quillabamba	Chuncho	n
P4	Quillabamba	Chuncho	n

2 Methods and Material

2.1 Sampling

Samples of *Cacao* beans (seeds of *Theobroma Cacao*) were taken during fermentation: In 2017, a preliminary experiment was run in Ivochote/Peru where specimen were obtained before start of the fermentation (day 0) and then daily until the fermentation was stopped at day 4. In 2018, 10 fermentations in four different regions were sampled. These samples were augmented by an additional 4 samples from commercially imported cacao from four different bags (by Peru Puro, Frankfurt, Germany; two roasted and two unroasted). For an overview, see table 2.1.In order to study sampling error, 2 – 4 increments from prescribed positions in the fermentation box (reactor) were obtained according to a sampling plan. Increments kept apart for the following analyses in order to allow a rough guesstimate of the sampling uncertainty.

In the laboratory, the field sample increments were further divided into 6 portions à 20 beans each for chemical reference analysis plus 100 beans for a cut test per fermentation-day (i. e., 25 – 50 beans per increment, depending on the number of increments available for the fermentation-day in question). Approximately 25 beans per fermentation-day were kept for possible further experiments. The large remainder of the material undergoes further roasting experiments and sensory analysis.

Laboratory sample splitting was done in a 2-stage process.First, an in-house constructed sample divider was used to obtain a pre-set fraction of the sample containing at least the number of beans required for chemical analysis and cut test. From these, the required number of beans for each portion was *randomly* selected.

2.2 Spectroscopic Measurements and Reference Analyses

Portions for chemical reference analyses were peeled and ground. NIR spectra between 3600 and 12500 cm^{-1} of $2\times$ approximately 1 ml of the ground material were measured with a Bruker MPA (Bruker, Ettlingen/Germany) NIR spectrometer at 8 cm^{-1} spectral resolution.

Afterwards, the 2017 material material was de-greased and extracted with methanol. In order to keep track of analytical error, this was done in duplicate as was the actual chromatography run.

2.3 Design of Experiments and Statistical Analysis

Simulation In order to see the effects of the different experimental designs proposed by Bainbridge [1], we set up a simulation comparing these designs and their analysis by mixed models for two common scenarios comprising 3 levels of data (e. g. primary/field samples, portions/aliquots, and measurements):

1. the number of possible measurements at the lowest level is limited — a situation frequently encountered with time-consuming wet-chemical reference analyses
   Here, we simuate 48 measurements in total, and in consequence according to the chosen design 12, 16, and 24 primary samples with 1 or 2 aliquots/portions each.

2. the number of available samples at the topmost level is limited – a situation rather typical for studies of biological systems.
   The simulation has 12 primary samples and in consequence 48, 36 and 24 measurements in total (again 1 or 2 aliquots).

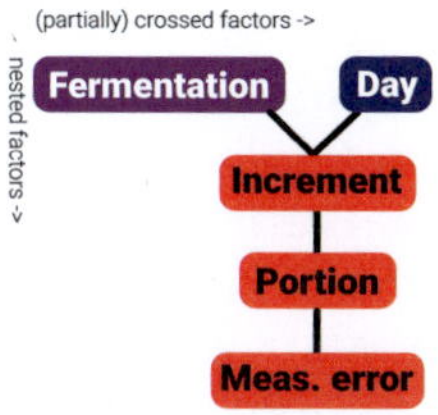

(a) Hasse Diagram.

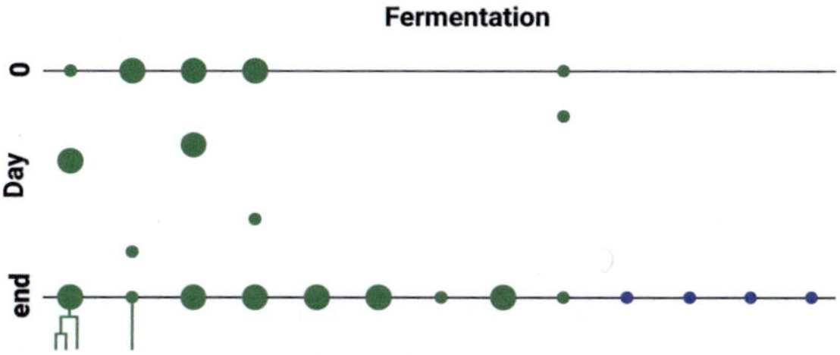

(b) Tabular representation.

Figure 2.2: Thinned out design of experiments for reference analyses (2018 material): **(a)** The Relationship among the various factors. Blue: Fixed factor fermentation *Day*, red: Random factors (confounders: The field sampling variance in *Increment*, biological bean-to-bean variance covered in *Portion* as well as the analytical random error in the lab procedure *Meas.error*), violet: Factor *Fermentation* comprises a mix of fixed and random factors such as random batch-to-batch variation as well as possible variation due to region and variety (fixed factors) which cannot be separated due to lack of samples. **(b)** Thinned-out experimental plan showing the partially crossed design for factors *Fermentation* and *Day* chosen for reference analysis. Large dots mark *Fermentation* × *Day*s where two increments and for one of them two portions were selected. For the other increment as well as for the *Fermentation* × *Day*s marked with small dots, a single portion was randomly chosen (depicted exemplarily for the two leftmost *Day n* samples). Blue circles mark the samples taken from commercially imported cacao.

The data is univariate random with mean zero and variance 1 for each of the data hierarchy levels (nested random factors). We obtain point estimates as well as bootstrapped 95 % confidence intervals for the 3 variance components via mixed models [2]. The simulation comprises 1000 runs per scenario.

Reference Analysis DoE The 2017 material was analysed with a fully nested design employing 3 portions ("Aliquot") × double extraction × double chromatography.

As the capacity for wet chemical processing and reference analysis is limited, we employ a thinned-out design for selecting samples for a first round of reference analyses of the 2018 material: Of the 44 available *Fermentation* × *Days* 30 are selected so that all fermentation are covered always with samples of the fermented cacao beans. Where samples were taken throughout the fermentation, a sample from before the start as well as an additional sample from one randomly selected day in between was chosen in addition. This reduces the number of portions to be analyzed from 264 to 45, i.e. about 17 % while still retaining the ability to check the approximate contribution of variance of the various confounders. This procedure takes into account the relations of the various factors, namely that *Fermentation* and *Day* are partially crossed while *Increments* are nested within *Fermentation* × *Days*, *Portions* within *Increments* and further random errors characterizing the analytical method are nested within *Portions*, see the so-called Hasse-Diagram (see [3] for a discussion).

Based on these reference analyses, a preliminary calibration will be performed which then allows to select a further portions for reference analysis in order to achieve a good and roughly uniform coverage of calibration samples in concentration space.

All statistical analyses were performed in R [4], in particular using packages hyperSpec [5] for handling of the spectra and [2] for mixed models.

3 Results

Simulation In a preliminary simulation experiment, we compared the three experimental designs described by Bainbridge [1]. We observe (fig. 2.3) across all designs and for both scenarios that the variance at the uppermost level is somewhat overestimated while the lower two variance components (factors) are on average well estimated (though the lowermost is slightly underestimated with the inverted nested design). As expected, the fully nested design allows precise estimation of the variance of the lowermost factor, but the uppermost variance estimation is highly imprecise: The median confidence interval width for the estimated standard deviation of the topmost factor is about twice the actual standard deviation. In comparison, the staggered nested design achieves a slight improvement on the confidence interval width for the uppermost factor which comes at the cost of slightly worse precision in the variance estimates of the middle and lowermost factors.

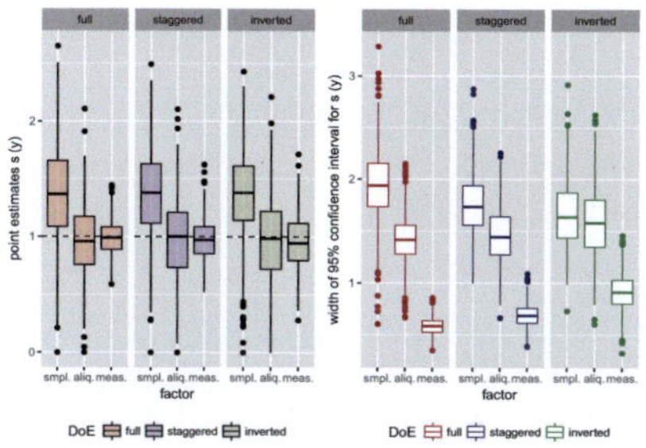

(a) Measurement-limited scenario.

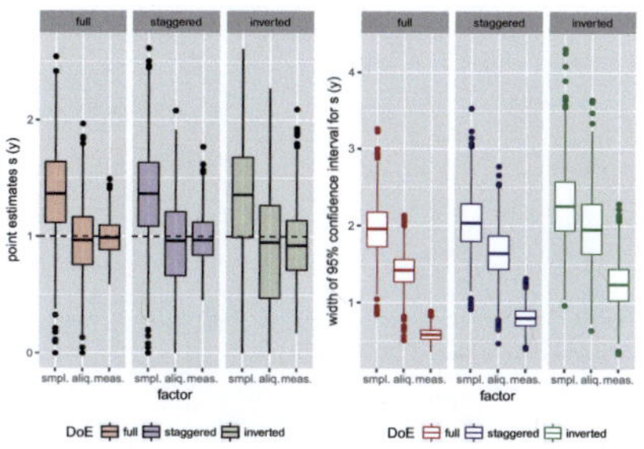

(b) sample-limited scenario

Figure 2.3: Results of the mixed-model variance component estimation for fully nested, staggered nested and inverted nested designs on simulated data. Filled boxes: Distribution of point estimates and empty boxed distribution of the estimated confidence interval widths for the 1000 simulation runs.

The inverted design goes further in this direction and achieves similar precision for the middle and uppermost factors. The lowermost factor is still estimated with higher precision. These trends are similar for both scenarios. However, in the measurement-limited scenario the confidence interval width for the topmost factor improves from fully nested over staggered nested to inverted nested design, whereas for the sample-limited scenario all variance estimates get increasingly imprecise in the same order. This is plausible considering that here for few samples, the already limited number of measurements is progressively decreased, while for the measurement limited scenario the number of measurements stays constant and is distributed across a larger number of primary samples.

We conclude that the inverted nested design can be recommended in situations where the total number of measurements, i. e. the number of samples at the lowermost factor, is limited. If, instead the number of primary samples (of the topmost factor) is the limitation, a fully nested design yields the maximum amount of information that can be gotten from the limited number of samples.

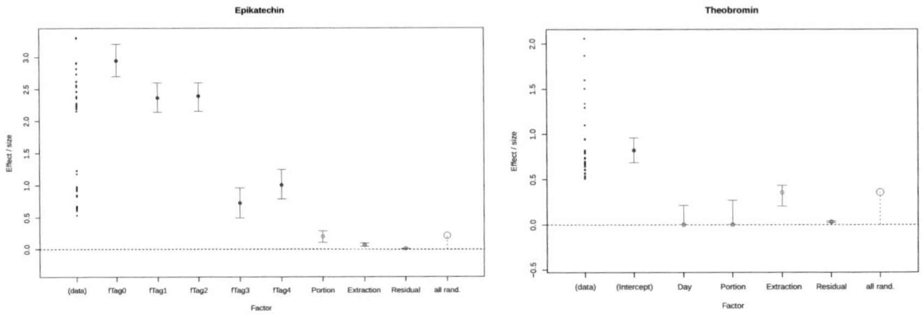

Figure 2.4: Changes in epicatechin content **(left)** during fermentation (blue, fixed factor) and comparison with the order of magnitude of 3 levels of confounding variance (red, random factors) in the laboratory processing chain for the reference analyses: Variance due to the laboratory sample division including the biological bean-to-bean variance, random error of the extraction procedure and random error of the actual chromatographic reference analysis. Theobromin content **(right)** is not expected to vary significantly during the fermentation, so only one fixed factor (blue) for the content is modeled and the day-to-day variation is considered mostly random field sampling error.

Epicatechin content mixed model. Fig. 2.4 shows preliminary results for analyte epicatechin of the 2017 material. Epicatechin is a secondary plant metabolite and antioxidant. Epicatechin content decreases during fermentation with a marked drop after day 2, i. e. when fermentation conditions are changed from anaerobic to aerobic. In addition to the fixed factor describing the temporal development, we extracted variance estimates for three confounding factors nested within our samples. The uppermost factor, *Portion* contains variance due to each portion consisting only of a limited number of cacao beans and is thus related to the biological bean-to-bean variance. We also observe that the random errors contributed by further steps in the laboratory processing (*Extraction*) and actual measurement (*Residual*) are each considerably smaller than the next. This corresponds well with the rule of thumb that the measurement noise contributed by modern analytical equipment is typically much smaller than the random errors introduced in the processing of samples and that sampling is often the step introducing most uncertainty. We conclude that the most efficient use of further experimental resources here is to examine more and/or larger portions of cacao beans. In other words, upcoming work (2018 material) will benefit from examining more primary samples and in turn switching to an inverted nested design.

In contrast, for theobromine, we found that the extraction procedure was the main contributor of uncertainty, and in consequence focus our attention to that part of the analytical procedure. Note that here we also see the difficulty in estimating variance components further up in the data hierarchy: *Portion* (bean-to-bean variance) and *Day* (field sampling error) cannot reliably be estimated. This is a direct consequence of the large variance at *Extraction* level.

4 Acknowledgements and Contributions

Financial support of the project "CocoaChain" (IGF 169 EN/3) by the AIF (Arbeitskreis industrielle Forschung) and FEI (Forschungskreis der Ernährungsindustrie) is highly acknowledged.

The authors thank H. Balster (2017), M. Nourisson, C. Bahmann (2018) and K. Zug (2017 + 218) for taking the field samples, as well as F. Tietz for prepraring the extracts for chromatographic analysis of the 2017 material and M. Harke for helpig with preparation of the lab samples, NIRS and some reference measurements.

The field sampling plans were constructed by AK (2017) and CBe (2017, 2018). Lab sample division, randomized measurement plans, selection of samples for reference analysis and statistical/chemometric analyses including the simulation study were performed by CBe. The reference analysis plan and methodology was devised by AK, CBö and CBe. Chromatographic analyses were set up, optimized and performed by MG and CBö.

5 Summary

Inverted nested designs of experiments allows us to construct a highly thinned-out set of samples for reference analys while for NIR spectroscopy where sample preparation and measurement are less time-consuming and more suitable for automation we employ a fully nested design. Both designs allow estimation of nested variance components, but the inverted nested design in our case runs time-consuming wet-lab preparation and reference analysis for only $\approx 17\,\%$ of the available samples in the first round of a two round calibration strategy. In a second round, more samples will be added and their selection will be guided by the preliminary calibration obtained in the first round.

We use mixed models to estimate contributions of several sources of uncertainty, i. e. confounding factors, along the analytical-chemical processing chain of the samples. This in turn allows us to focus further work where it is most efficient: On the respectively largest source of uncertainty in the processing chain.

References

1. T. R. Bainbridge, "Staggered, nested designs for estimating variance components," *Industrial Quality Control*, pp. 12–20, 1965.
2. D. Bates, M. Mächler, B. Bolker, and S. Walker, "Fitting linear mixed-effects models using lme4," *Journal of Statistical Software*, vol. 67, no. 1, pp. 1–48, 2015.
3. G. W. Oehlert, *A First Course in Design and Analysis of Experiments.* (W. H. Freeman), 2010. [Online]. Available: http://users.stat.umn.edu/~gary/book/fcdae.pdf
4. R Core Team, *R: A Language and Environment for Statistical Computing*, R Foundation for Statistical Computing, Vienna, Austria, 2018. [Online]. Available: https://www.R-project.org/
5. C. Beleites and V. Sergo, *hyperSpec: a package to handle hyperspectral data sets in R*, 2018, r package version 0.99-20181022. [Online]. Available: http://hyperspec.r-forge.r-project.org

Absorption properties of lipid-based substances by non-invasive fast mid-infrared imaging

Tim Kümmel[1,4], Tobias Teumer[1,3], Patrick Dörnhofer[1], Steffen Manser[1,4], Sascha Heinrich[1], Andreas Hien[1,4], Jürgen Marx[2], Frank-Jürgen Methner[3], Matthias Rädle[1], and Björn Wängler[4]

[1] Mannheim University of Applied Sciences,
Center for Mass Spectrometry and Optical Spectroscopy,
Paul-Wittsack-Str. 10, 68163 Mannheim, Germany
[2] Scanovis GmbH,
An der Königsbach 8, 56075 Koblenz, Germany
[3] Technische Universität Berlin,
Institute of Food Technology and Food Chemistry,
Seestraße 13, 13353 Berlin, Germany
[4] University of Heidelberg,
Medical Faculty Mannheim,
Theodor-Kutzer-Ufer 1-3, 68167 Mannheim, Germany

Abstract In this study, we present a new optical non-contact measurement method, which is based on general characteristics of a flying-spot scanner. The focus is on the mapping of lipid-based substances, especially the scanning of fingerprints. The assessing of human fingerprints is conducted by using two lasers emitting in different selected wavelengths. Images generated by using these wavelengths comprise absorption information of the examined sample. By using image-processing and conversion algorithms, the lipid-based substances in the detected image section could not only be captured, but also displayed three-dimensionally. The setup of the optical scanning method presented here utilizes the mid infrared region, especially the wavelength range between 3 µm up to 4 µm. It was optimized in order to scan an area up to 50 cm^2, with a spatial resolution of 20 µm and a data rate of 300 kS/s. Our data shows that mapping of human fingerprints can be performed by using the described method. Furthermore, a processing of the data set results in topographical information.

Keywords: Mid-infrared, scanning, absorption, lipids, non-invasive, human fingerprint, papillary ridge.

1 Introduction

Dactyloscopy is a person identification method recognised by science and jurisprudence. It deals with the recording and evaluation of human fingerprints [1]. Dactyloscopic marks are unique, unchangeable and classifiable. Due to these properties, they are particularly suitable for use in forensic technology. Dactyloscopic marks at crime scenes are created in the form of imprints, both latently by the excretion of skin's own substances, e.g. finger fat, and by the transfer of exogenous substances. Fingerprints are created by the papillary ridges on the fingertip. Each finger has a unique pattern. These patterns remain the same for a lifetime. Fingerprints can be classified into different pattern types. For this purpose, part of the total imprint is determined as the pattern area [2]. Forensically, general papillary line progressions and conspicuous structures are investigated [2,3]. These structures form the basis for the dactyloscopic proof of identity. The shape and position of the features in relation to each other represent primary importance [3]. Conspicuous structures on fingertips such as scars, wrinkles and furrows are also examined.

In practice, optical [4,5], physical [4] and chemical methods [6,7] are used to make a fingerprint visible. In certain specific cases, it is possible to search and to visualize finger marks in one step, however the original mark is destroyed in this approach [4–8]. In other cases, the finger mark securing can be performed at the same time [6]. The (substrate) material, its surface condition and its substance are important components in the selection of a suitable process [5].

The detection of finger marks by means of optical methods is contactless and non-destructive [4,5]. However, this method demands long measurement periods [9]. Therefore, we present a non-contact scanning measurement method providing fingerprints for rapid visualization and measurement data for further digital processing.

2 Materials and methods

The middle infrared (MIR) scanning setup used here is based on a flying-spot scanner [10]. The measurement setup basically consists of two lasers, a focusing unit, an agile mirror system and a detector (Figure 3.1). The laser beams are deflected one-dimensionally by the agile mirror unit. The sample is displaced orthogonally to the deflected laser beam by means of a translation stage. This method and confocal signal acquisition reduce image distortion. The maximum measuring area is 50 cm^2 with a spatial resolution of 20 µm. The sample is scanned at a sampling rate of 300 kS/s. At this scanning speed, the maximum measuring area is scanned within 50s. This is the measurement time for each individual laser.

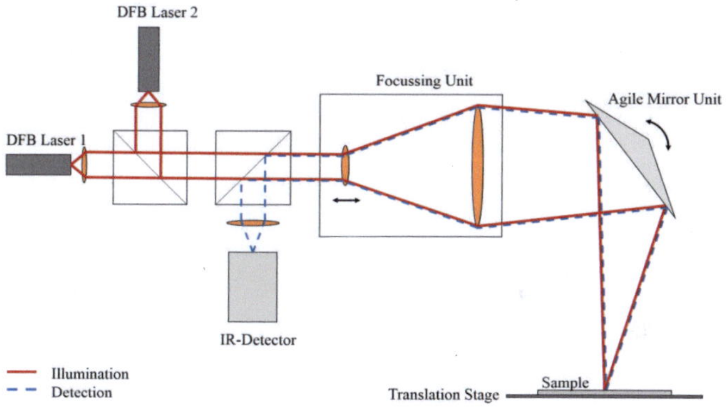

Figure 3.1: Schematic representation of the MIR scanner. The laser beam is focused on the sample by the agile lens unit (Focussing Unit). The laser light is deflected by the agile mirror unit orthogonally to the deflection direction of the laser beam, the translation stage operates. The detector is confocally mounted at the optical path of the laser light.

The acquired measurement data are sorted by complex algorithms and assembled as a measurement image. The resulting and calculated measurement images represent the absorption properties at the measuring target. The following sequence of measurements demonstrates the absorption properties of human body fat. On these, 3-dimensional finger fat marks are created. Each individual has a different concentration of body fat [11], so a standard reference is used. Wool wax (adeps lanae anhydricus; antioxidant = max. 200 ppm BHT), in its properties approximately similar to human body fat, is used for reference.

3 Theory/Calculation

The Lambert-Beer law in MIR spectroscopy is applied to the MIR scanner presented here. The measured absorption A is composed of the negative decadic logarithm of the transmission T (Equation 3.1). In this case, the absorption is proportional to specific sample concentration c, thickness of sample material d and material-dependent extinction coefficient ϵ [12].

$$A = -log_{10}(T^2) = -log_{10}\left(\frac{I_{Laser1}}{I_{Laser2}}\right)^2 = \epsilon c d_{Substance} \tag{3.1}$$

The transmission T is determined by the ratio of the two lasers. Here, the exponential dependence of the transmission represents the twofold sample passage of the laser light. This is comparable to DRIFTS (diffuse reflectance infrared fourier transform spectroscopy). The absorption A can be calculated by transforming the transmission. Based on this assumption, conclusions can be drawn as to the measured material thickness $d_{Substance}$ at a constant concentration c of a substance.

In theory, the aim is to set one of the two lasers (Laser 1) to the wavelength of a transmission minimum and to set the second laser (Laser 2) to a transmission maximum. Since the extremes are accompanied by rapid increases or decreases of the flanks, it is not always possible to adjust the laser exactly to theoretical values. Therefore, it is of decisive importance to locate a laser (Laser 1) within a band exhibiting an increased absorption coefficient. In contrast, the second laser (Laser 2) has to be located in a range that has a lower absorption level than Laser 1. In Figure 3.2, the lasers used in this work are highlighted in the spectral transmission range of fat and oil. Laser 1 is set to the wavelength λ = 3417 nm (2926 cm^{-1}) and laser 2 to the wavelength λ = 3584 nm (2797 cm^{-1}). The samples presented in Figure 3.2 show the C-H vibration the lasers are adjusted to. The adjusted wavelengths therefore absorb substances from triglicerides in combination with long-chain fatty acids.

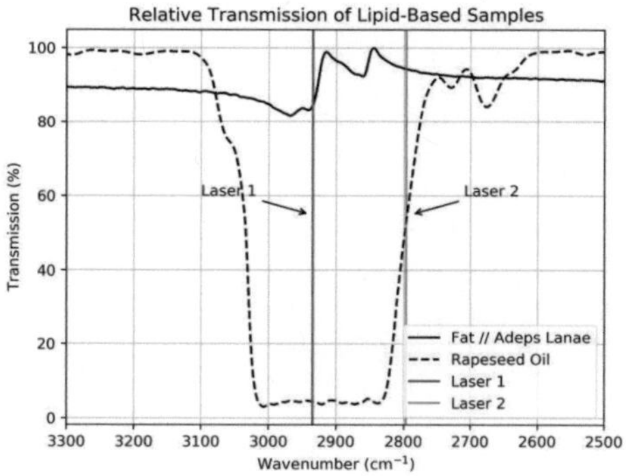

Figure 3.2: Relative transmission of fat (Adeps Lanae) and rapeseed oil. Both exhibit differences in transmission at wavenumbers from 2500 cm^{-1} to 3300 cm^{-1}. The wavenumbers of the lasers are located in the band between 2980 cm^{-1} and 2700 cm^{-1}. Laser 1 assumes the wavenumber 2926 cm^{-1} and Laser 2 the wavenumber 2797 cm^{-1}.

4 Results and Discussion

The scan results presented in Figure 3.3 depict the measurement results with the MIR scanner in raw data format. Figure 3.3a) represents the scan result for Laser 1 with wavelength 3417 nm. In contrast, Figure 3.3b) shows the scan result of Laser 2 with wavelength 3584 nm. Figure 3.3c) shows the calculated transmission T^2 as an enlarged section of the measurement results. Based on this calculated and magnified section, the profile thickness is evaluated and demonstrated in the following.

These measurement data are linked to a calibration subsequently (Figure 3.4). Hence, the absorption of different layer thicknesses is determined for both wavelengths. After scanning the layer thicknesses, a linear calibration curve of wool wax fat is generated. The related relative transmission of both laser wavelengths as a function of the penetration depth is shown in Figure 3.4a).

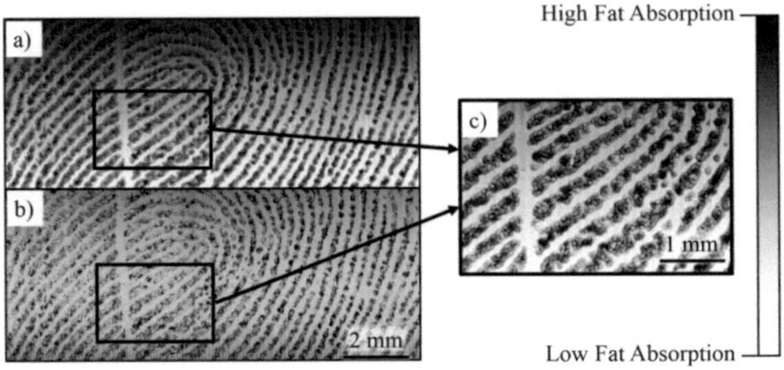

Figure 3.3: Scan result of a human fingerprint. a) Scan of the fingerprint with wavelength 3417 nm. b) Scan of the fingerprint with wavelength 3584 nm. c) Section of calculated transmission T^2(zoomed).

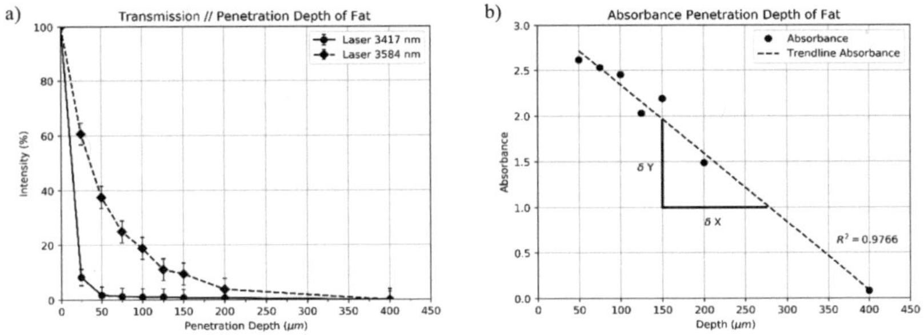

Figure 3.4: Depiction of the penetration depth for fat. a) The intensity of the two wavelengths decreases for both lasers with increasing penetration depth. b) Determination of the penetration depth using a calibration model for fatty substances (especially finger fat).

By determining the penetration depth, a calibration is performed enabling the penetration depth to be assigned to an absorption value. The absorption is obtained by applying Equation 3.1 to the determined penetration depth values as shown in Figure 3.4a). As a result, a linear calibration curve can be generated for layer thicknesses between 25 µm and 400 µm (Equation 3.2). The calibration curve is illustrated in Figure 3.4b). For a penetration depth less than 25 µm, the coefficient of determination decreases, this is equivalent to a nonlinearity in a calibration curve associated with it. This is due to insufficient absorption at this layer thickness. In contrast, the maximum penetration depth to be determined is limited to 200 µm. The signal-to-noise ratio (SNR) is not sufficient for data processing at higher penetration depths. Theoretically, a penetration depth of up to 400 µm could be achieved. By linking the calibration curve with Lambert-Beer, an unknown layer thickness d can be calculated from the measured absorption A (Equation 3.3).

$$A = md + b \tag{3.2}$$

$$d = \left(\frac{A - b}{m}\right) \qquad \rightarrow with : m = \frac{\delta d}{\delta A} = \frac{d_n - d_{n-1}}{A_n - A_{n-1}} \tag{3.3}$$

This mathematical method is applied to the following scan results of Figure 3.3c). A layer thickness is assigned to each image pixel and related to the absorption information. This results in a topographic image of the fingerprint. Image processing procedures are used to assign a visual colour to each layer thickness. The calculated scan result is presented in Figure 3.5.

Figure 3.5 demonstrates an average profile height between 150 µm and 200 µm for this fingerprint. In addition, it is shown that the background of the fingerprint is eliminated by calculating the absorption differences (Equation 3.1). For improved visualization, Figure 3.6 shows the height profile on the plot line (PL) marked in Figure 3.5. The widths, the heights and distances between the papillary ridges can be determined directly from such a plot.

Figure 3.6 indicates that the papillary ridge and the associated heights of the finger fat are not contiguous. In addition, peaks are recognizable by increasing and decreasing profile heights. This is due to direct reflections from structural changes. To reduce the associated increase in intensity and the resulting falsified profile height, a smoothing filter (Savitzky-Golay filter) can be superimposed on the structure [13]. This generates a more homogeneous continuous height of the fingerprint. The disadvantage is the elimination of interrupted structures within the papillary ridge and the associated loss of information.

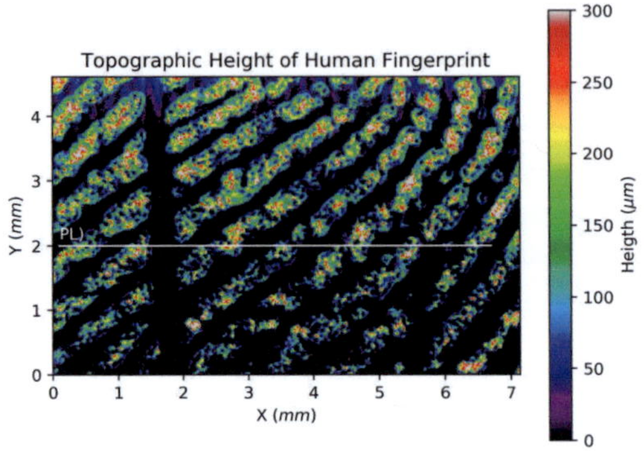

Figure 3.5: Absorption image of the fingerprint depending on the depth information of the fat layer. The plot line (PL) indicates a single line represented in Figure 3.6.

5 Conclusions

In this work we proved the possibility to visualize fingerprints with the MIR scanner and assign topographic information to the generated image. A scan rate of 300 kS/s in combination with the spatial scan resolution of 20 μm provides fast, high spatial resolution scan results. Here we rely on the absorption measurement with two different wavelengths, exhibiting absorption differences of long-chain C-H bonds. In addition, we demonstrated a calibration method based on known mathematical correlations that enables conclusions about the thickness of finger mark. The results are generated immediately from the measured data. Thus, the fingerprint is displayed as an image with height information of the analyzed sample. The resulting image, containing the 3-dimensional structures of the fingerprint, can thus be passed on to the forensic analysis [3] for further processing. Further test series for thin layers (< 25 μm) will be performed with nonlinear regressions. In addition, an adjustment of smoothing algorithms is necessary, depending on the examined structure and associated interruptions. Fingerprints on various surfaces have to be checked as well.

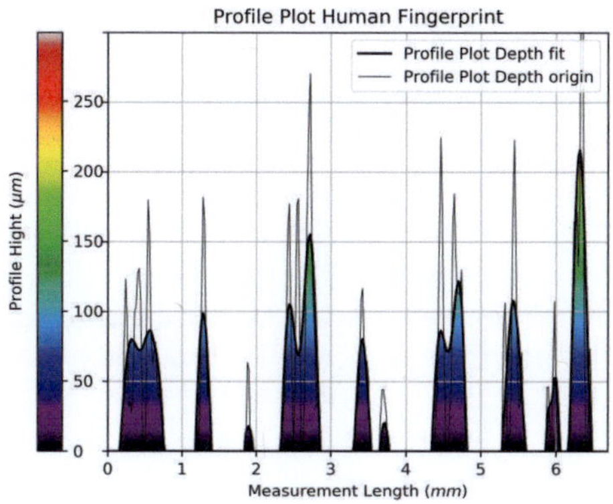

Figure 3.6: Representation of the profile depth of the scanned fingerprint as an original and smoothed detection signal with colour assignment of the profile height.

Furthermore, this measuring principle is applicable to oil and associated oil residues. For this purpose, a new calibration has to be performed for the respective oil, as this absorbs differently in liquid form as shown in Figure 3.2.

Acknowledgement

The German Federal Ministry of Economics and Energy (BMWi), supported by the Association of Industrial Research Associations (AiF Project GmbH, Grant No: ZF4168604TS8, ZF4560205TS8), have sponsored this project. The authors would also like to thank the Karl-Völker-Stiftung (KVS) for its financial support.

References

1. S. C. Dass, "Fingerprint-based recognition," *International Statistical Review*, vol. 81, no. 2, pp. 175–187, 2013.
2. A. de Jongh, A. R. Lubach, S. L. Lie Kwie, and I. Alberink, "Measuring the rarity of fingerprints patterns in the dutch population using an extended classification set," *Journal of forensic sciences*, 2018.
3. N. Yager and A. Amin, "Fingerprint verification based on minutiae features: a review," *Pattern Analysis and Applications*, vol. 7, no. 1, pp. 94–113, 2004.
4. P. H. R. Ng, S. Walker, M. Tahtouh, and B. Reedy, "Detection of illicit substances in fingerprints by infrared spectral imaging," *Analytical and bioanalytical chemistry*, vol. 394, no. 8, pp. 2039–2048, 2009.
5. C. G. Worley, S. S. Wiltshire, T. C. Miller, G. J. Havrilla, and V. Majidi, "Detection of visible and latent fingerprints using micro-x-ray fluorescence elemental imaging," *Journal of forensic sciences*, vol. 51, no. 1, pp. 57–63, 2006.
6. M. Najdoski, S. Oklevski, and G. Stojković, "A simple chemical method for visualization of sebaceous fingerprints on unfired cartridge cases by prussian blue deposition," *Russian Journal of Applied Chemistry*, vol. 88, no. 11, pp. 1896–1901, 2015.
7. Y. Wang, J. Wang, Q. Ma, Z. Li, and Q. Yuan, "Recent progress in background-free latent fingerprint imaging," *Nano Research*, pp. 1–20, 2018.
8. R. Bhargava, R. S. Perlman, D. C. Fernandez, I. W. Levin, and E. G. Bartick, "Non-invasive detection of superimposed latent fingerprints and inter-ridge trace evidence by infrared spectroscopic imaging," *Analytical and bioanalytical chemistry*, vol. 394, no. 8, pp. 2069–2075, 2009.
9. J.-H. Rabe, D. A. Sammour, S. Schulz, B. Munteanu, M. Ott, K. Ochs, P. Hohenberger, A. Marx, M. Platten, C. A. Opitz *et al.*, "Fourier transform infrared microscopy enables guidance of automated mass spectrometry imaging to predefined tissue morphologies," *Scientific reports*, vol. 8, no. 1, p. 313, 2018.
10. N. Ramanujam, J. Chen, K. Gossage, R. Richards-Kortum, and B. Chance, "Fast and noninvasive fluorescence imaging of biological tissues in vivo using a flying-spot scanner," *IEEE Transactions on biomedical engineering*, vol. 48, no. 9, pp. 1034–1041, 2001.
11. R. Ostlund Jr, J. Yang, S. Klein, and R. Gingerich, "Relation between plasma leptin concentration and body fat, gender, diet, age, and metabolic covari-

ates," *The Journal of Clinical Endocrinology & Metabolism*, vol. 81, no. 11, pp. 3909–3913, 1996.

12. D. Swinehart, "The beer-lambert law," *Journal of chemical education*, vol. 39, no. 7, p. 333, 1962.
13. P. A. Gorry, "General least-squares smoothing and differentiation by the convolution (savitzky-golay) method," *Analytical Chemistry*, vol. 62, no. 6, pp. 570–573, 1990.

Spatially resolved ingredient detection in spice mixes using 3D convolutional neural networks

Johannes Anastasiadis, Wolfgang Krippner,
and Fernando Puente León

Institute of Industrial Information Technology (IIIT),
Karlsruhe Institute of Technology (KIT),
Hertzstr. 16, 76187 Karlsruhe, Germany

Abstract A method using spectral information to detect substances in mixtures is given. The presented convolutional neural network is using three-dimensional convolutions to process hyperspectral images. Reflectance values can be fed directly into the network and are not preprocessed. Due to the architecture, the neural network performs a spatially invariant operation. Detection performance is demonstrated by a dataset containing spice mixtures.

Keywords: Hyperspectral image, optical measurement, convolutional neural network, three dimensional.

1 Introduction

Optical measuring methods play a major role in food investigation as non-contact and non-destructive methods. They can be used for quality assessment, e.g., by detection of undesired substances. Hyperspectral images (HSIs) are often used if normal colour images do not provide enough information. While the latter only comprise three colour channels (red, green, and blue), the former contain up to several hundred wavelength channels [1]. By this additional information, conclusions about material properties can be drawn [2–4].

Artificial neural networks have been very successful in recent years. Convolutional neural networks (CNNs) are particularly successful in image processing [5]. They are also used to process HSIs, but many approaches only perform a convolution along either the spectral dimension [6] or the spatial dimensions [7, 8]. To merge information of the two domains, several approaches exist in literature. The mayor amount uses fully connected layers [9, 10]. In [11] three-dimensional (3D) convolutions are used, however, fully connected layers are needed in later process steps to get an output value for each pixel.

In our approach, 3D convolutions are used in the first layers to process information of spatial and spectral domain simultaneously. The following layers use 1×1 two-dimensional (2D) convolutions along the spatial dimensions, which can be regarded as a full connection along the spectral dimension. Because of this, the approach is spatially invariant. Furthermore, we do not require any preprocessing such as principle component analysis, used in [7], for instance. Therefore, the CNN uses the complete information provided by HSIs. In this work, the approach is applied to detect substances in mixtures. The aim is to decide whether a substance is comprised in a pixel.

The rest of the paper is organized as follows: Basics of neural networks and CNNs are given in Section 2. In Section 3, the structure of the proposed CNN is described. The results attained by this CNN are shown in Section 4. A brief summary is given in Section 5.

2 Convolutional neural networks

Neural networks are black box modelling approaches in which data is used to learn non-linear functions. The basic modules of neural networks are called neurons, which are inspired by biological neurons. Each neuron consists of several inputs and one output. The neurons are connected with each other, and those connections can end up in loops. Feedforward neural networks, as used in this work, have no loops, and neurons are arranged in layers. Every neuron of each layer is connected to every neuron of the previous layer and to every neuron of the following layer. There are no connections within a layer. Such layers are called fully connected layers. A single layer is described mathematically as

$$\mathbf{h} = \varphi(\mathbf{W}\mathbf{x} + \mathbf{b}), \tag{4.1}$$

where $\mathbf{h} \in \mathbb{R}^K$ is the output and $\mathbf{x} \in \mathbb{R}^J$ the input of the layer. The matrix $\mathbf{W} \in \mathbb{R}^{K \times J}$ contains the weights the input is multiplied by, and $\mathbf{b} \in \mathbb{R}^K$ is the bias vector. There is one scalar bias value for every neuron. The non-linear activation function φ is applied elementwise. It is necessary to enable approximations of functions different from linear functions. The neural network is trained by adjusting weights and biases for every layer. This is done by optimizing an objective function. In most cases, a gradient-based method is used. The gradient can be backpropagated through the neural network to update all parameters [12].

In CNNs, layers are not fully connected. Instead, the input is convolved with a filter kernel which is much smaller than the input. Afterwards, a scalar bias value is added. This leads to some advantages in image processing. First of all, the same kernels are used for every region of the image, and therefore, the operation is spatially invariant. The spatially resolved approach proposed in this work exploits this fact. Furthermore, spatial relations of data are taken into account. Last but not least, significantly less parameters are required compared to fully connected layers. Only the parameters describing the kernels and the biases have to be trained.

An important aspect to understand CNNs in image processing is the treatment of channels or feature maps. A convolution is performed along spatial dimensions (two dimensions for colour images). This is done with a different filter kernel for every channel (or feature map). The output of this operation is added up to a new feature map. This is done with several filter kernel sets to produce more feature maps and, thereby, extract more features [5]. It can be interpreted as the network is convolutional along spatial dimensions and fully connected in spectral direction (see Fig. 4.1). A bias value is added to every pixel of the output feature maps afterwards. In Fig. 4.1, a 2D convolution is shown as an example.

In most CNNs, pooling layers, in which local clusters of values are combined to a single value (see e.g. [13]), are also used. Commonly, and also used in this work, is max pooling, which propagates only the largest value to the next layer. Using pooling leads to less parameters in the subsequent layers, which results in shorter training times and reduces the risk of overfitting.

All basics provided in this section are used in the next section to design a CNN consisting of convolutional and pooling layers.

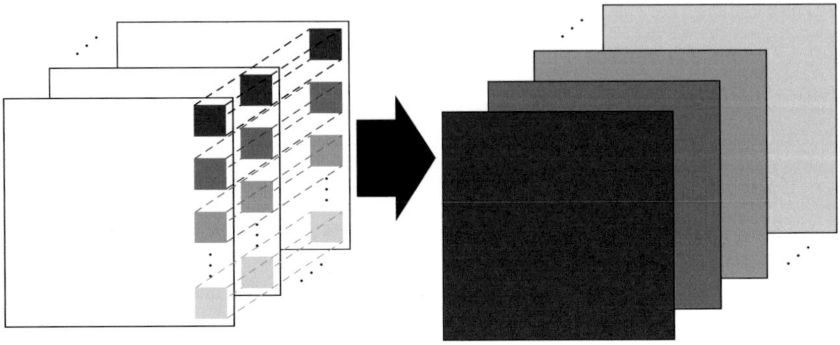

Figure 4.1: Principle of a convolutional layer (without bias): The input data has C_{in} feature maps of size $H_{\text{in}} \times W_{\text{in}}$ pixels. The input is convolved with C_{out} sets of filter kernels. Each set contains one filter kernel for each input feature map, respectively. The sum of the convolutions of each filter kernel set results in an output feature map. Therefore, the output has C_{out} feature maps of size $H_{\text{out}} \times W_{\text{out}}$ pixels.

3 Neural network design

The input to the CNN are HSIs, which can be interpreted as 3D data cubes with two spatial and one spectral dimension. To each element of the cube a reflectance value is assigned.

The proposed CNN consists of two parts: The first part exploits 3D convolutions along the spatial and the spectral dimensions resulting in 3D feature maps. After each convolutional layer, a pooling layer along the spectral dimension is used. For this reason, the spatial resolution is preserved (see Fig. 4.2, first row). This design allows for getting the position of a detected ingredient. In the second part, the 3D feature maps are transformed into 2D feature maps by splitting them along the spectral dimension (see Fig. 4.2, second row). For example, W feature maps of size $X \times Y \times \Lambda$ lead to $W \cdot \Lambda$ feature maps of size $X \times Y$ after splitting. It is an important step in our approach to combine 3D convolutions in the first few layers with 2D 1×1 convolutions along the spatial dimensions in the subsequent layers (see Fig. 4.2). The 3D con-

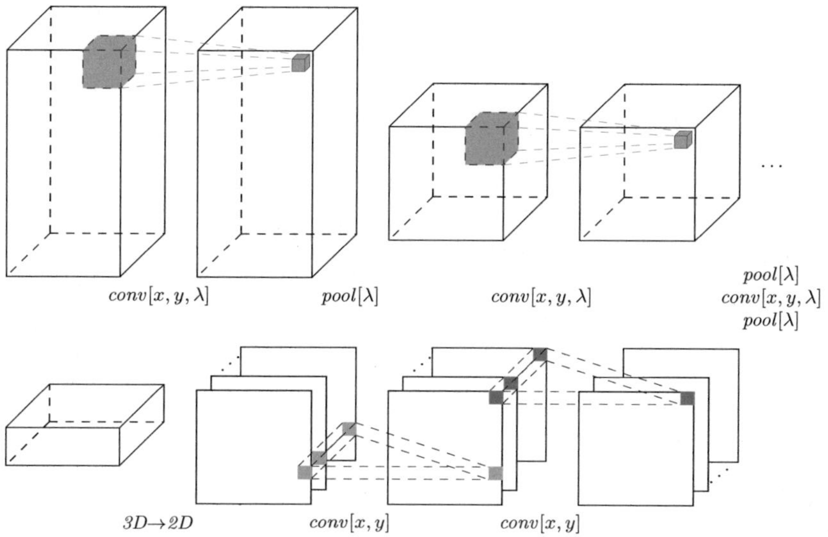

Figure 4.2: Proposed net architecture: The first three layers are 3D convolutional (*conv*) layers followed by a pooling layer (*pool*), respectively. The last two layers perform a 2D 1×1 convolution. The square brackets define along which dimensions the operation is performed (spatial dimensions: x, y, spectral dimension: λ). Note that only one 3D feature map is shown for each step.

volutional layers are used for feature extraction. The 2D convolutional layers operate as fully connected layers along the spectral dimension.

The CNN produces a map for each ingredient as an output. Having the same spatial resolution as the HSI, the maps may indicate where an ingredient is detected. The operation performed by the CNN is spatially invariant because only convolutions are performed along the spatial dimensions (see Section 2).

The CNN shown in Fig. 4.2 is evaluated in Section 4 with different filter sizes. In all experiments, batch normalisation is performed before activation [14], and in each layer, the sigmoid function $\sigma : \mathbb{R} \rightarrow \mathbb{R}$ is used as the activation function:

$$\sigma(z) = \frac{1}{1 + \mathrm{e}^{-z}} \,. \tag{4.2}$$

4 Experimental results

The dataset used for training and evaluation of the CNN was acquired in the image processing laboratory of the Institute of Industrial Information Technology. Eleven spices were mixed in 155 mixtures, each consisting of maximum four different spices. Hyperspectral images of the mixtures with a spatial size of 24×24 pixels were acquired. They consist of 91 wavelength channels from 450 nm to 810 nm. A white balance was applied in order to ensure reflectance values as data. The dataset is divided into a training and a test set with a ratio of 2:1. The input of the CNN are HSIs, each containing several mixtures (see Fig. 4.2).

To evaluate the result F-measure F is used. It is the harmonic mean of precision PRE and recall REC:

$$F = \frac{2 \cdot PRE \cdot REC}{PRE + REC}, \tag{4.3}$$

$$PRE = \frac{TP}{TP + FP}, \qquad REC = \frac{TP}{TP + FN}. \tag{4.4}$$

In Equation (4.4) TP is the number of true positives, FP the number of false positives, and FN the number of false negatives.

In the following sections, several parameter sets are compared with both each other and with the method provided by *Makantasis et al.* [7]. This method only uses 2D convolutions along the spatial dimensions. The spectral dimension is treated as a channel or feature map, respectively (see Fig. 4.2, second row). To account for the spectral information, Randomized Principal Component Analysis (R-PCA) is used along the spectral dimension. For all experiments, the sizes of the filter kernels were chosen according to [7].

4.1 Comparison of filter sizes

In this section, an appropriate size for the filter kernels used in the 3D convolutional layers is determined. The size of the 2D filter kernels is restricted to 1×1. In Table 4.1, the number of output feature maps for all experiments is given. The number of input channels is one.

Table 4.1: Number of the output feature maps of each convolutional layer: The number of input feature maps of the next layer corresponds to the number of output feature maps of the current layer, except for layer 4. Here, the number of input feature maps is the number of output feature maps times the size of the spectral dimension of layer 3 (see Section 3).

Convolutional layer	1	2	3	4	5
Output feature maps	16	32	64	66	11

In Figure 4.3, several filter kernel sizes are compared using F-measure. The proposed CNN performs better than the method by *Makantasis et al.* [7] for all filter sizes. This implies that using 3D convolutions works better than using R-PCA for feature extraction. The inclusion of spatial information ($w_{xy} > 1$) improves the results, but depends on the setting of the edge lengths w_{xy} and w_{λ}. If the spatial edge lengths are chosen too large, the performance decreases. The best result is achieved for $w_{\lambda} = 7$ and $w_{xy} = 3$. In addition, for smaller w_{λ} larger w_{xy} are beneficial.

The detection performance depends not only on the parameters, but also on the input data. Therefore, all the spices contained in the mixtures are evaluated separately in the next section.

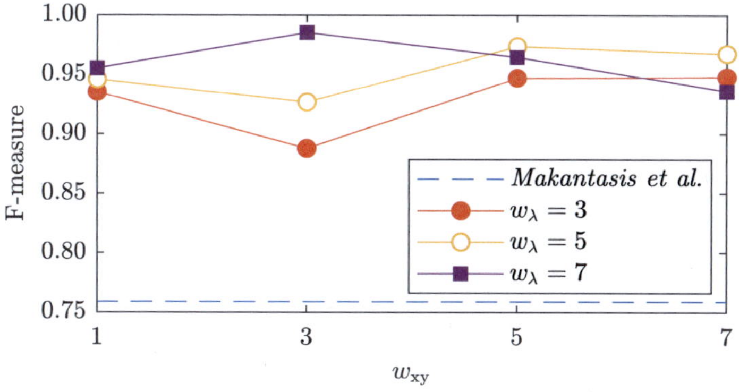

Figure 4.3: F-measure values for several filter sizes used in the first three layers (see Fig. 4.2, first row). Here, w_{xy} is the spatial edge length and w_{λ} the spectral edge length of the filters. The method by *Makantasis et al.* [7] is used for comparison with the recommended filter sizes.

4.2 Comparison of spices

Figure 4.4 shows F-measures calculated separately for all spices. In particular, the method in *Makantasis et al.* [7] and the proposed CNN using two different parameter sizes are investigated. The parameter size that leads to the overall best F-measure, and the one that leads to the best F-measure including no spatial information (see Fig. 4.3) are compared.

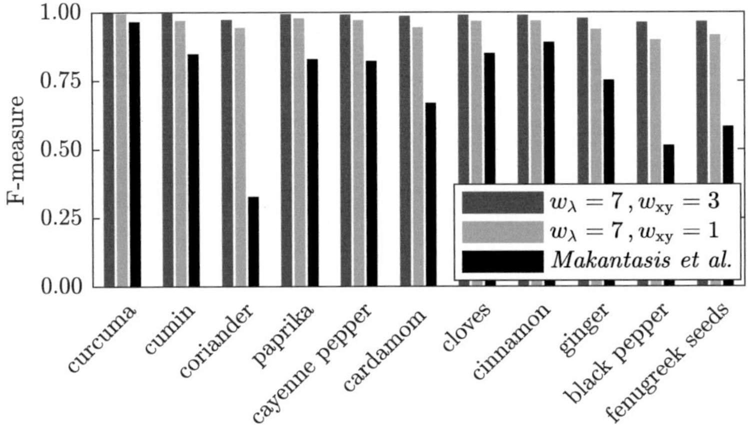

Figure 4.4: F-measure for all spices using the best filter size settings. *Makantasis et al.* [7] with recommended settings is displayed for comparison.

The accuracy of spice detection variates between the spices for all methods. The method by *Makantasis et al.* [7], using R-PCA and only 2D convolutions, shows much higher variance than our method, using 3D convolutions. Besides, spices, which bad detection performance using the method by *Makantasis et al.* [7], also lead to lower F-measure values using the proposed CNN. We conclude that the accuracy of the detection depends on the input data. This has much stronger implications for *Makantasis et al.* [7] than for our method.

5 Summary

A CNN architecture using only convolutional layers along the spatial dimensions has been presented. It was shown that the our CNN design performs a spatially invariant operation and maintains the spatial resolution of the input HSI. The CNN is performing 3D convolutions in the first few layers to extract features and is fed with non preprocessed reflectance values. In this work, the goal of the CNN is to detect ingredients in spice mixtures and was evaluated by a dataset created in our laboratory. Including spatial information in the 3D convolutional layers leads to the best results. Nevertheless, the size of the neighbourhood should not be chosen too large. A CNN, which uses only 2D convolutions along the spatial dimensions [7] and R-PCA for preprocessing, is outperformed by the proposed CNN. The accuracy of detection depends on the considered spice mixtures for all evaluated methods.

In the future, the CNN could be trained with data containing the quantitative amount of spices and used to determine the amount of ingredients.

References

1. A. Gowen, C. O'Donnell, P. Cullen, G. Downey, and J. Frias, "Hyperspectral imaging – an emerging process analytical tool for food quality and safety control," *Trends in Food Science & Technology*, vol. 18, no. 12, pp. 590–598, 2007.
2. S. Bauer, J. Stefan, and F. Puente León, "Hyperspectral image unmixing involving spatial information by extending the alternating least-squares algorithm," *tm – Technisches Messen*, vol. 82, no. 4, pp. 174–186, 2015.
3. W. Krippner, S. Bauer, and F. Puente León, "Considering spectral variability for optical material abundance estimation," *tm – Technisches Messen*, vol. 85, no. 3, pp. 149–158, 2018.
4. W. Krippner, S. Bauer, and F. Puente León, "Optical measurement of material abundances in mixtures incorporating preprocessing to mitigate spectral variability," in *OCM 2017*. Karlsruhe: KIT Scientific Publishing, 2017, pp. 87–96.

5. Y. LeCun and Y. Bengio, "Convolutional networks for images, speech, and time series," *The handbook of brain theory and neural networks*, vol. 3361, no. 10, 1995.

6. W. Hu, Y. Huang, L. Wei, F. Zhang, and H. Li, "Deep convolutional neural networks for hyperspectral image classification," *Journal of Sensors*, vol. 2015, 2015.

7. K. Makantasis, K. Karantzalos, A. Doulamis, and N. Doulamis, "Deep supervised learning for hyperspectral data classification through convolutional neural networks," in *Geoscience and Remote Sensing Symposium (IGARSS), 2015 IEEE International*. IEEE, 2015, pp. 4959–4962.

8. S. Yu, S. Jia, and C. Xu, "Convolutional neural networks for hyperspectral image classification," *Neurocomputing*, vol. 219, pp. 88–98, 2017.

9. Y. Chen, Z. Lin, X. Zhao, G. Wang, and Y. Gu, "Deep learning-based classification of hyperspectral data," *IEEE Journal of Selected topics in applied earth observations and remote sensing*, vol. 7, no. 6, pp. 2094–2107, 2014.

10. C. Chen, F. Jiang, C. Yang, S. Rho, W. Shen, S. Liu, and Z. Liu, "Hyperspectral classification based on spectral-spatial convolutional neural networks," *Engineering Applications of Artificial Intelligence*, vol. 68, pp. 165–171, 2018.

11. Y. Li, H. Zhang, and Q. Shen, "Spectral-spatial classification of hyperspectral imagery with 3d convolutional neural network," *Remote Sensing*, vol. 9, no. 1, 2017.

12. D. E. Rumelhart, G. E. Hinton, and R. J. Williams, "Learning representations by back-propagating errors," *nature*, vol. 323, no. 6088, pp. 533–536, 1986.

13. A. Krizhevsky, I. Sutskever, and G. E. Hinton, "Imagenet classification with deep convolutional neural networks," in *Advances in neural information processing systems*, 2012, pp. 1097–1105.

14. S. Ioffe and C. Szegedy, "Batch normalization: Accelerating deep network training by reducing internal covariate shift," *CoRR*, vol. abs/1502.03167, 2015.

Process control for the food production

Theresa Hanf, Sven Leuchs, and Dirk Nüßler

Fraunhofer Institue for High Frequency Physics
and Radar Techniques FHR,
Fraunhoferstraße 20, 53343 Wachtberg

Abstract In the following paper, measurements of shortcrust samples at different temperatures with high frequency electromagnetic waves are disclosed. Therefore, a vector network analyzer is used to generate high frequency signals. The samples were heated with a standard kitchen oven. Based on the measured signal parameters (magnitude and phase), the baking process can be characterized. Thereby a process control in baking operation is possible.

Keywords: Process control, radar, electromagnetic waves, dough, shortcrust, dielectric, transmission, inline measurements.

1 Introduction

The production of foodstuffs like bakery products or convenience food is even in a fully automated production line a critical task. Food is a natural product and based on the provenance, the weather conditions during the growth phase and the production process, the ingredients, the quality of the base products the final products variate in quality and consistence. It is the expertise of the people involved in the production process who are compensating these fluctuations inside the process-chain. Without the expertise of these bakers, brewers, confectioners and others who change the process minimal based on their expertise the quality of the final product will decrease considerable. However, even these experts have problems when changes inside the machine park influence the quality. The heating ramp of a backing oven can change depending on the age of the machine or the running time. The question is whether high frequency sensors can support this production process. When an electromagnetic wave transmits a dielectric material, the attenuation and the transition time of the wave are affected based on the dielectric constant of the material under investigation. In the microwave region the humidity inside the product normally dominates the behavior of the material, simplified a wet product attenuates the signal more and causes a greater delay than a dry product. But also smaller effects like the fermentation process of dough causes a detectable change. In this paper, we have a closer look on the baking process itself and investigate how the temperature profile influences products like cookies. The idea behind these measurements is not to control the temperature inside the oven but the speed of the production line. To fulfill this task, it is necessary to investigate the behavior of the dough during the baking process and to develop a measurement configuration, which allows us to measure inside the oven.

2 System concept

One of the main advantages of the microwave frequency range is the fact that electromagnetic waves in this frequency range penetrate the most non-conducting materials. This effect can be used to guide a signal, which is generated outside the oven through the isolating walls of the baking oven. Typically, the signals are guided by cables or metallic waveguide. For the measurements, a frequency-modulated continuous-wave radar (FMCW) is the best choice to perform the measurements. FMCW is a short-range measuring radar, which is normally used to determine the distance between the radar and an object. In this radar systems, a signal of a known frequency is generated which is modulated over a fixed period and varies up and down in frequency. A part of the transmitted signal is coupled out and compared with the received signal. Echoes from a target are then mixed with the transmitted signal to produce a beat signal, which will give the distance of the target after demodulation. Frequency difference between the received signal and the transmitted signal increases with delay, and hence with distance. The delay is not based only on the distance, a change of the propagation constant also creates a change of the measured distance. The water concentration typically dominates the value of the dielectric constant but during the baking several events occur that can be used to control the baking process. In a first step, it is necessary to check which of the events causes a dominant change in the dielectric constant in the microwave frequency range. The main challenge is that the reduction of the water concentration in the dough superimpose the smaller changes. The main events which typically occur during a baking process are the melting of the fats, the dying of the microorganisms, gases form and expand, sugar dissolves, proteins, including enzymes, coagulate, starches gelatinize, liquids evaporated, browning occurs on crust, changes occur to nutrients and pectin breaks down. Some of the events like the dying of microorganisms cause no relevant change of the dielectric constant in the microwave region. Others like gases which are formed or the evaporation of liquids cause a strong change of the dielectric constant and can be used to steer the baking process.

3 Measurements

The measurement setup for performing the dielectric measurements of attenuation and phase consists of a vector network analyzer for generating the electromagnetic waves in a given frequency range. The used VNA is able to generate frequencies up to 67 GHz. However, this frequency is too low for analyzation of the shortcrust. Therefore, two extender modules were used to generate frequencies in a range from 75 to 110 GHz. The investigated sample is measured in a transmission setup (see figure 5.1 a). In this, the electromagnetic waves of the given frequencies were emitted via a dielectric drop antenna through the sample and are received with another drop antenna on the backside of the sample. Due to the elliptical shape of the antenna a planar phase front directly behind the antenna is formed (see figure 5.1 b and c). Therefore, it is possible to arrange both antennae near to the sample. The antenna has a 3 dB-aperture of around 5 °. For the experiments, a simple shortcrust is used as sample. The shortcrust consists of three main ingredients: one part of sugar, two parts of fat, and three parts of flour. Margarine is used as a substitute for fat. The dough is rolled out to a thickness of 3 and 6 mm and cut into several squares (50x50 mm). Then the shortcrust samples were baked for 13 minutes (or 18 minutes for 6 mm cookies). Therefore, a standard kitchen oven with lower and upper heat mode was used. Every minute the dough was taken out of the oven and the transmission through the dough was measured in amplitude and phase over the complete frequency band from

(a) Transmission setup (b) Elliptical shaped antenna (c) Antenna field pattern

Figure 5.1: Measurement and antenna setup.

75 to 110 GHz. The measurement results of different same sized samples of the same manufacturing process show strong variation. Figure 5.2 exemplary shows the attenuation of 10 different shortcrust samples at a heating time of 7 minutes. Due to the strong inhomogeneity in the temperature distribution in the used oven, it cannot be guaranteed that every sample has the same temperature and this leads to different transmission behavior. Accordingly, multiple shortcrust samples were measured and the results are averaged. It should be noted, that for every measurement at a discrete time step of the heating process time a new set of shortcrust samples is assembled to reduce undesired effects of cooling and reheating of the samples. For the first view, measurements with different oven temperature and different sample thickness are done. The results are shown in figure 5.3, in the form of a relative attenuation with respect to the attenuation at time step t_0. The results are averaged over all sample measurements (as mentioned above) and over all frequencies too since there are no significant changes in the frequency range over time visible. An oven temperature of 150 °C and 200 °C is used. The curves show some characteristics. First the attenuation of the samples increase until a spot where the attenuation reaches a maximum value. From this point on the attenuation more or less linearly decreases until the attenuation later remains on a saturated level. This behavior is reproduced by several measurements. As mentioned above the dough consists of sugar, margarine and flour. The amount of water in margarine is about 20 %. By heating the dough, the water inside the dough is also heated. The dielectric losses of water

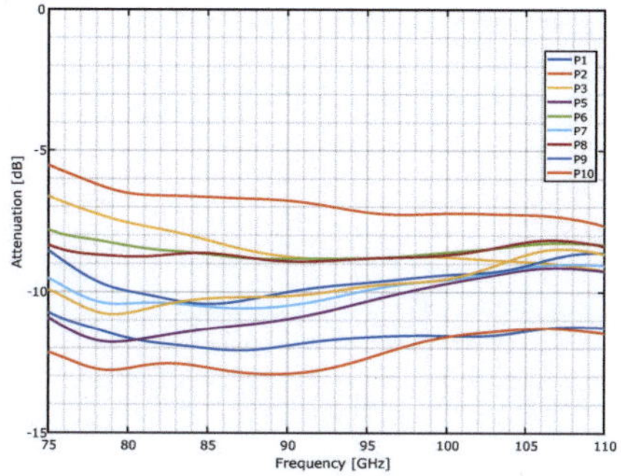

Figure 5.2: Measured attenuation of 10 different shortcrust samples at a time step.

increase with temperature [1] and the attenuation increases. This process is depicted in the measurement data. On the other hand the water evaporates due to the increasing temperature and at one point the attenuation decreases. In the measurement plot the increase in attenuation corresponds with a decrease of the curve (relative attenuation) and vice versa. During the series of measurements, it appeared that the dough samples were noticeably mushy at the beginning. Only from a temperature of about 90 °C, the dough pieces took a firmer structure. This temperature coincide with the measured dip in the attenuation curve. From this point on the outer structure of the samples becomes drier (from the outside to the inside) and the attenuation decreases. Figure 5.4 shows the surface temperature of the samples in the heating process. After a strong raise the temperature slowly reaches a level with a quite smaller raise. The dip in the curve for the experiments with an oven temperature of 150 °C is at 5 minutes. By increasing the temperature to 200 °C the dip moves to a shorter time (3 minutes). By increasing the temperature the described process is accelerated and the characteristic dip is reached faster. Increasing the thickness from 3 to 6 mm leads to a massive increase in attenuation, due to more mass of the sample. The dip does not change its position, at least not within the limits of 1-minute measurement quantization. The thickness of the sample seems to have a lower influence on the bounding water mechanism.

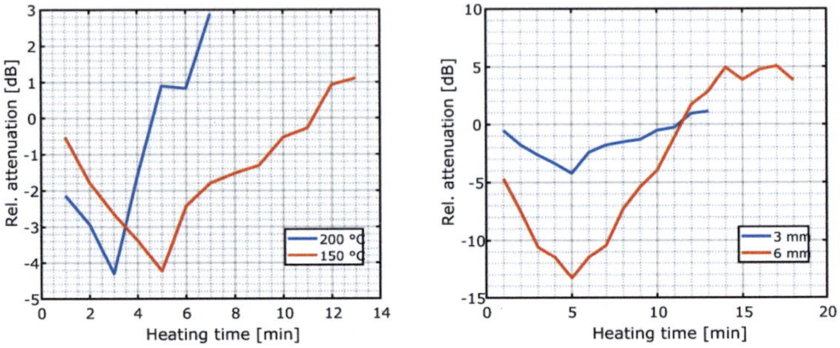

(a) 150 °C vs 200 °C (b) 3 mm vs 6 mm

Figure 5.3: Influence of heat and thickness variation on relative attenuation.

Besides the process of water getting free and evaporated, more processes take place. These are, amongst other things, the volume increase due to expanding gases in the shortcrust, denaturation of proteins and starch gelatinization [2]. To investigate these processes, further series of measurements with different dough compositions were carried out.

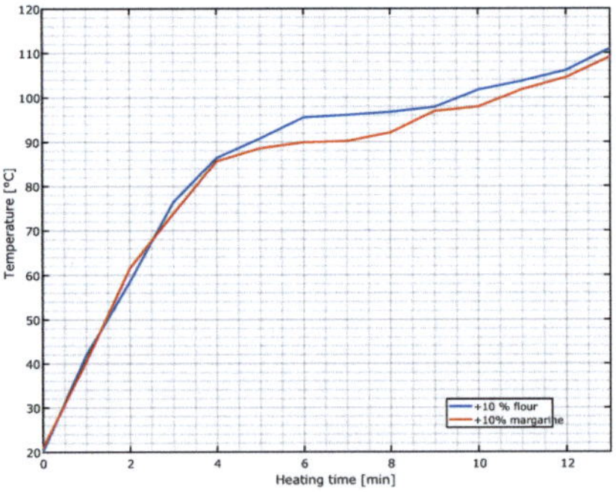

Figure 5.4: Surface temperature of dough pieces during heating process.

First, the amount of margarine is increased by 10 % and in another series the amount of flour is also increased by 10 %, to see the effects on the measured data (attenuation and phase shift). The results of these measurements are shown in figure 5.5. In the left plot of figure 5.5 the relative phase shifts (with respect to the shift at time step t_0) of the measurements are shown. In the first minutes the phase barely changes. The phase shift of an electromagnetic wave refers to a time delay, which is caused by longer transit time through a material. After around 4 minutes, the phase changes abruptly. After the beginning of heating the samples, the core temperature begins to increase more and more. This leads to an expansion of any gases that are inside the dough, for example air that has come into the dough by kneading. In the experiments, this expansion was observed after around 3-4 minutes. Due to the physical expansion of the samples, the phase abruptly changes. After the abrupt change, the phase constantly changes with a lower slope. By changing the composition of the shortcrust and adding more flour and margarine, the phase and attenuation results for flour and margarine look very similar. In contrast, the abrupt phase shift in the standard recipe is quite higher, the slope after has quite the same shape. The dip in attenuation curve occurs for the changed composition 1 minute prior to the standard composition. By adding more flour the dough becomes a higher contents of starch and proteins. Its shape is a little bit more brittle since the amount of water is less and the gelatinization process is more difficult. By adding more margarine the amount of water and fat increases. With increasing temperature the attenuation of fat generally increases, but the changes are not that high [3]. Regarding the measurement curves there are some visible effects by changing the composition of the dough. To make a more accurate statement of which processes have which influence on the transmission behavior, more measurements have to be performed, for example with more different compositions. In general, it should be noted that there are several points that affect the measurements. It has been found that the dough pieces do not all have the same transmission behavior due to manufacturing variations after production. This error is attempted to counteract by averaging the measured data. Furthermore, in the oven used, no constant nor uniform heat distribution can be ensured, so that the dough pieces do not all have the same temperature or temperature distribution. In addition, it can not be guaranteed that the dough pieces all have the same thickness, since the production was done by hand. All these sources of error influence the measurement and impede the interpretability.

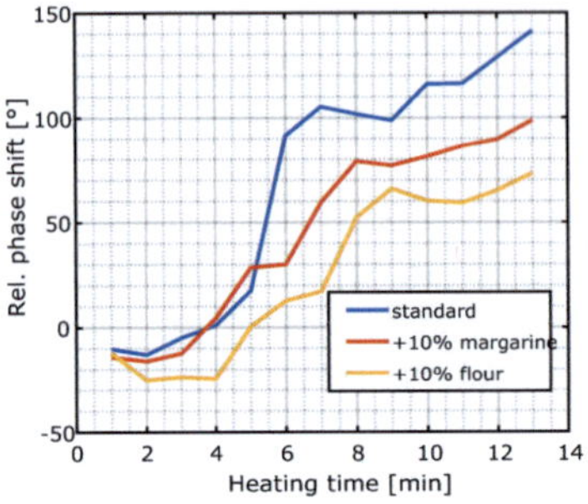

(a) Relative Phase

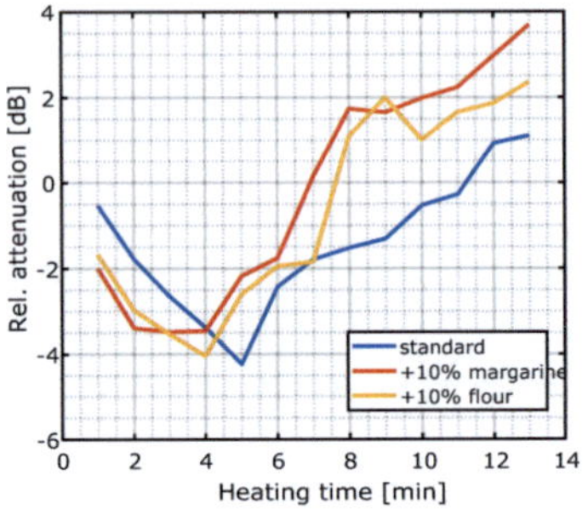

(b) Relative Attenuation

Figure 5.5: Measurement data for different dough compositions.

4 Summary

The results of the paper demonstrate that different events during the baking process can be observed in the microwave region by measuring the phase and amplitude behavior of a transmitted electromagnetic signal. These events are for example the volume increase due to expansion of gases, denaturation of proteins and starch gelatinization. The investigations have shown that a baking process can be mapped in the attenuation and phase behavior of electromagnetic waves. The measured curves show some characteristics that can be used for controlling the baking process and predict its completion. Typically the presence of water dominates the influence on the dielectric properties. To analyze the influence of the other processes several measurements with adapted compositions of dough were performed. The results between the standard prescription and the adapted prescriptions have similarities as well as differences. On the basis of the measurements carried out, however, no statement can yet be made as to which processes have which influence on the dielectric properties of shortcrust. It is necessary to perform more measurements to further specify the behavior of these influences.

References

1. A. Von Hippel and A. Labounsky, "Dielectric materials and applications," in *Artech House microwave library*, 1995.

2. W. Edwards, "The science of bakery products," in *The Royal Society of Chemistry*, Cambridge, June 2007.

3. S. Ryynänen, "The electromagnetic properties of food materials: A review of the basic principles," in *Journal of Food Engineering, Issue 26, pp. 409-429,* 1995.

Using hybrid information of colour image analysis and SWIR-spectrum for high-precision analysis of construction and demolition waste

Petr Kuritcyn[1], Katharina Anding[1], Elske Linß[2], and Gunther Notni[1]

[1] Ilmenau University of Technology, Faculty of Mechanical Engineering, Department of Quality Assurance and Industrial Image Processing, Gustav-Kirchhoff-Straße 2, 98693 Ilmenau

[2] Bauhaus-University Weimar, Faculty Civil Engineering, F. A. Finger Institute of Building Materials Science, Geschwister-Scholl-Straße 8, 99423 Weimar

Abstract This paper discusses the accuracy improvement of automatic analysis of construction and demolition waste (CDW) by using the combination of image analysis and spectral information. This means using the combination of methods of image processing, methods of spectral analysis and methods of supervised learning. The classification performances in colour images and also in SWIR-spectrums showed, that we have to use a combination of these two components in a combined feature vector to improve the accuracy of analysis. Investigations on hybrid information from colour images and SWIR-spectrums were done and compared with the separate usage of these information sources.

Keywords: Construction and demolition waste, machine learning, image processing, spectral analysis, hybrid information.

1 Introduction

Construction and demolition waste (CDW) are one of the biggest waste flow in Germany with around 68 million tons per year [1]. At the same time, the rate of the recyclable amount in producing of high-quality materials like recycling concrete and recycling asphalt is still relatively low, with 14 million tons per year (20.7%). For recycled masonry aggregates and recycled mixed aggregates, the lowest recycling rates are found because of the high heterogeneity and the mineral admixtures. Therefore, the desired reuse of these materials is very difficult. An important limitation factor is here the composition and heterogeneity of the material. The materials from the dismantling of buildings can be very heterogeneous in its material composition, depending on the origin, the method of dismantling and the processing. Recycled aggregates are characterized in the context of the quality assurance with respect to various structural parameters as well as the material composition. The latter is determined by a manual sorting analysis at relatively small sample sizes and is on the one hand very time-consuming and on the other hand strongly subjective. On the basis of the parameters and the material composition, the possibilities of utilization or possible fields of application are defined. The quality control is the prerequisite for obtaining the product status. Quality-controlled products have better chances on the market and thus lead to an image gain for the building material recycling industry and to a better utilization of given resources. This requires processes for the analysis of recycled aggregates, which provide precise, rapid and, above all, representative results. There are no method or device is developed or in common use, which allows a high performance recognition of all possible ingredients of CDW to realise an automatically and exactly analysis of CDW samples in context of the guidelines to reach a high quality product for building industry.

The results of own investigations by using image processing technics in colour images [2], [3] and spectral analysis methods in SWIR-spectrums [4], [5] showed, that there is a possibility to improve the accuracy of analysis by combining these two information sources in one feature vector as basis for classification. So investigations in colour images, SWIR spectrums and combined hybrid-information were done and then compared with each other.

We used pre-engineered system from project "Autopetrographie" with a 3CCD-line-scan camera to capture colour images and the SWIR spectrometer Polytec PSS 2120 with an InGaAs detector and a range of 1100 to 2100 nm to record spectrums of the CDW classes. In our classification routine we used supervised machine learning classifiers [6], feature selection methods and principal component analysis (PCA).

Previous investigations on a separate colour image dataset showed a total recognition rate of 96.9% and on a separate spectral dataset of 99.2% by using an optimized support vector machine with polynomial kernel. We did know that we have to combine the image information with the spectral information to enhance the recognition accuracy, because the best achieved total recognition rate of 99.2% is not good enough for an automatically analysis of the material composition of CDW. So we combined the separate feature vectors to a hybrid dataset for training and testing our supervised classifier.

2 Analysis of image information of several CDW classes

Like described in [3], we used the machine vision software HALCON to extract features from colour images. It results in feature vectors with more than 200 features (several contour, colour and texture features). Our previous investigations on colour images showed, that not all these features are relevant for classification and it's necessary to reduce the amount of redundant information by using feature selection methods. Several feature selection algorithms were tested and compared with each other.

All three feature selection methods (InfoGain, chiSquare, ReliefF) showed similar results. The application of ReliefF results in a smaller number of significant features in comparison to the two other methods, but results are better only for one class out of five. The InfoGain feature selection algorithm provide a good balance between accuracy and speed.

The classifiers svmPoly and MLP showed an underfitting by using a low number of features and an overfitting by using a high number of features. Recognition rates of classifiers are showing a plateau from 115 features. Further increase of the number of features resulted in a degradation of classification performance. It means that the first 115 features with the highest relevance are playing a crucial role for the recognition task.

Fig. 6.1 shows the number of specific features among the best. Texture and colour features are most frequently usable until 115 features (62 texture and 46 colour features among 115 best features based on InfoGain—filter, i.e. 94% of these features). It means that texture and colour feature are the most important features for recognition of CDW in images.

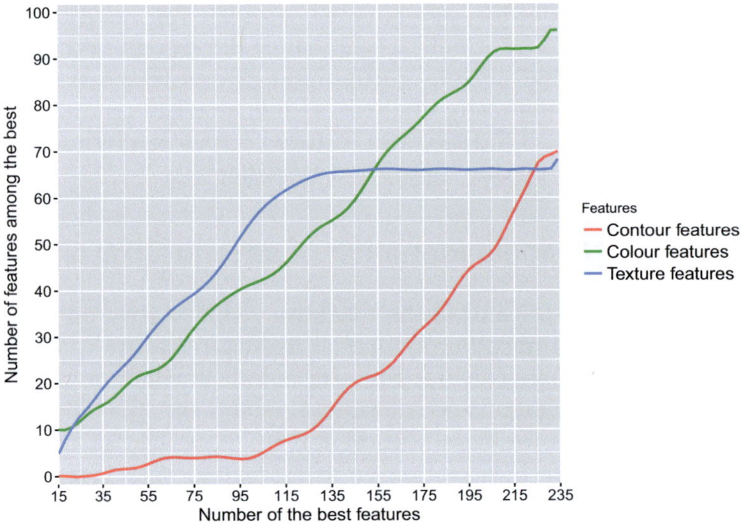

Figure 6.1: Number of specific features among the best, selected by InfoGain.

The application of principal component analysis on image dataset showed a degradation of results. Therefore, this method is not suitable for this task and leads to overcomplication of features.

3 Analysis of hybrid information of several CDW classes

In our investigations we used a dataset with similar size like in [5] (nearly 1100 samples out of the 8 superordinated classes: lightweight concrete, concrete, aerated concrete, sand-lime brick, dense and porous brick, gypsum and granite) (see Table 6.1). The image acquisition and spectrum record were done parallel and as a result, the feature vector of objects consists of both, the image and the spectral information for the same object.

The dataset was used for training and testing of different classifiers: SVM with different kernels, neural networks, decision trees and logistic regression classifier.

The recognition rates of all classifiers on hybrid dataset are increased between 1.6% (for Random Forest) and 11% (for MLP) in comparison to separate usage of spectral information from this dataset. On the contrary, the recognition rates decreased between 0.6% (for LogitBoost) and 6.6% (for Random Forest) in comparison to separate usage of image information from this dataset. A similar tendency was found on dataset with 8 material classes: increasing between 0.4% (for svmPoly) and 10% (for MLP) in comparison to usage of spectral information and decreasing between 0.3% (for LogitBoost) and 7.7% (for Random Forest) in comparison to usage of image information. It shows, that spectral part of datasets consists irrelevant information, which leads to degradation of results.

Table 6.1: Number of objects in hybrid dataset.

Material	Number of objects in dataset
Concrete	155
Granite	25
Gypsum	57
Lightweight concrete	200
Aerated concrete	225
Sand-lime brick	199
Dense brick	75
Porous brick	105

Feature selection and feature transformation methods are required to solve this problem. Investigations in [5] showed, that it is necessary to use PCA for the transformation of spectrum to achieve higher accuracy of analysis. The application of 16 first principal components for classification results in reduction of computation time in comparison to using of all 501 wavelength specific features and leads to increase of classifier performance.

The classifier svmPoly showed the highest recognition rate of 99.7% on hybrid dataset with 8 material classes. The classifier MLP is close with total recognition rate of 99.6%.

The current investigations on the spectral part of hybrid dataset have confirmed previous results – the optimal number of principal components is between 14 and 18 PC's.

After optimization of spectral part, there is one more possibility to improve results. Image part of hybrid dataset can be optimized as well. Feature selection methods were used for this task.

Some classifiers like MLP and svmLinear showed weak dependency of performance from number of used features. Other classifiers like svmPoly and LogitBosst showed worse results by using low number of features (underfitting) and by using high number of features (overfitting). Classifier Random Forest showed worse results by using high number of features.

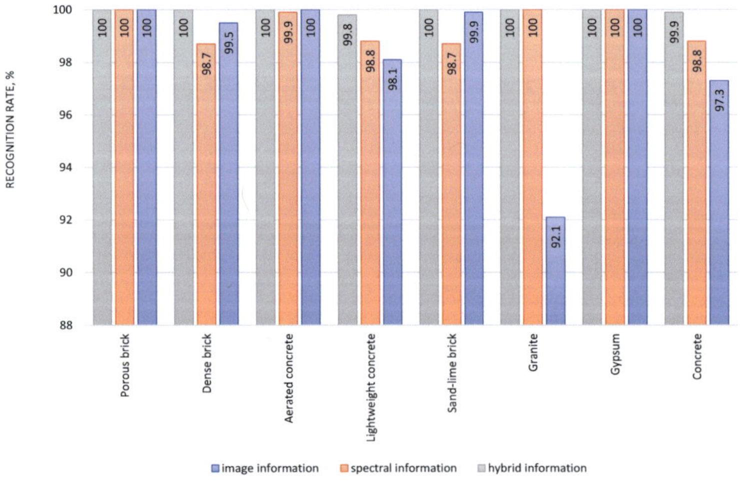

Figure 6.2: Comparison of the accuracy of the SVM with polynomial kernel for image, spectral and hybrid dataset (consists of 8 different material classes).

The two algorithms InfoGain and PCA were applied on the part of image information (120 features were selected) and spectral information (16 PC were selected) of hybrid dataset respectively. The best results showed the SVM classifier with polynomial kernel (Figure 6.2). In Figure 6.2 the comparison of the achieved accuracy of the SVM with polynomial kernel is shown for the image dataset, the spectral dataset and also for the combined hybrid dataset.

The achieved individual recognition rates based on the use of feature selection methods on the image feature vector and the principal component analysis on the spectral feature vector. In summary the individual recognition rates of the 8 classes achieved by SVMPoly for the hybrid dataset showed a very high recognition performance with nearly 100% (only for the classes lightweight concrete of 99.8% and for concrete of 99.9%).

4 Summary

The investigations on combined information (hybrid information) from colour images and SWIR-spectrums showed, that it's possible to improve the accuracy of analysis for the classes concrete, lightweight concrete, sand-lime brick and dense brick in comparison to the independent usage of the separate data. With application of the InfoGain feature selection on colour image part and PCA on spectral part of the data and using of a SVM classifier with polynomial kernel it's possible to achieve recognition rates of nearly 100% for all reviewed material classes. Most of them showed a 100% recognition rate due to relatively small dataset size. The results showed that a method for automatic recognition of all common CDW classes could developed, which allows a high performance recognition of all CDW classes to realise an automatically analysis of the material composition of CDW in context of the guidelines. It will be a reliable method for ensuring the quality of secondary building materials produced from construction and demolition waste.

Further investigations are planned for testing the method on a bigger dataset.

References

1. "Mineral construction waste – Monitoring 2014. Kreislaufwirtschaft Bau," Berlin, Tech. Rep., 2013.

2. K. Anding, E. Linß, H. Träger, M. Rückwardt, and A. Göpfert, "Optical Identification of Construction and Demolition Waste by Using Image Processing and Machine Learning Methods," in *14th Joint Int. IMEKO Symp.*, Jena, Germany, 2011.

3. P. Kuritcyn, K. Anding, E. Linß, and S. M. Latyev, "Increasing the safety in recycling of construction and demolition waste by using supervised machine learning," in *IMEKO Joint Symposium 2014 TC1 - TC7 - TC13 „Measurement Science Behind Safety and Security"*, Madeira, Funchal, September 2014.

4. "NIR-Sorting of CDW. Final report of AiF scientific project. AIF-KF 2155712," Bauhaus-University Weimar, Tech. Rep., 2013.

5. K. Anding, P. Kuritcyn, E. Linß, and S. M. Latyev, "Significant characteristics in VIS- and IR-spectrum of construction and demolition waste for high-precision supervised classification," in *OCM 2015 - 2nd International Conference on Optical Characterization of Materials*, Karlsruhe, Germany, March 2015.

6. M. Kuhn, "The caret Package," 2009.

Detection and classification of heterogeneous materials as well as small particles using NIR-spectroscopy by validation of algorithms

Xiaozheng Chen and Alexander Feil

RWTH Aachen University,
Department of Processing and Recycling
Wüllnerstr. 2, 52062 Aachen

Abstract Detection, characterization and sorting of plastics using Near-Infrared (NIR) Spectroscopy is State of the Art for plastic recycling processes. NIR active materials could be characterized according to the specific spectra of each material in the NIR spectrum. This works well for homogeneous materials, as they have known uniform spectra. For the detection of heterogeneous material and particles with smaller size than the resolution of NIR camera, the analysis becomes difficult due to mixed spectra. In this paper, the capturing of spectra information with a NIR camera takes place simultaneously with the optical detection with a VIS (Visible light) camera. The NIR spectra and VIS information are combined for the analysis of the mixed spectra, because the higher resolution of VIS camera contributes to a clear definition between the plastic materials and the background as well as between the selected materials. In order to determine the material composition, different kinds of mixed spectra of plastics with background as well as of plastic composition were detected and analyzed. The background is a conveyer belt made of black plastic, and the studied types of plastics are Polypropylene (PP), Polystyrene (PS), High-Density-Polyethylene (HDPE) and Polyvinylchloride (PVC). For the analysis, several algorithms will be developed and tested. In the end, a universal algorithm which performs well for all kinds of mixed spectra will be selected and improved.

Keywords: NIR-spectroscopy, resolution, analysis, sorting, heterogeneous material, Classification.

1 Introduction

Plastic is one of the most widely used materials in the industry. Detection, classification and sorting of all types of plastic materials are important processes in the recycling chain of plastics. The state of the art for the sorting of plastics is sensor-based sorting with Near-Infrared (NIR) spectra technology [1,2]. Different kinds of plastic materials show distinct spectra in the NIR wavelength area. According to a known specific reflection of different wavelength, the material could be detected and classified. The accuracy of NIR based sorting of plastics can be higher than 98 % with a throughput up to 6 tons/h [3]. However, the application of NIR classification is limited. In some cases, the detection of heterogonous material can be a challenge due to the mixed spectra, mainly because the pixels in the contact zones and at the object edges are compositions of two or more types of materials [4]. The spectra of these pixels are not unique anymore as pure material. Especially when processing small heterogonous particles, the recognition of these particles can result in a wrong classification due to low spatial resolution. In this context, the particle size for the detection with NIR technology is also limited. For example, during the quality-management-process of the Polyethylene terephthalate (PET) flakes, the flakes can be smaller than the resolution of NIR camera, the spectra are, accordingly, mixing of PET and background. Thus, the classification is not possible. In this study, different types of mixed spectra were analyzed. The pixels with mixed spectra are confirmed with the information from the VIS camera due to its higher resolution. The mixed spectra of various plastic materials with background has been captured and analyzed. Besides, the mixed spectra of contact zones of different kinds of materials have been investigated. Several algorithms were tested for the analysis in order to compare with each other and find out the most suitable one for the classification of mixed spectra. The aim of this research is to investigate the possibility of the detection and classification of heterogeneous material and particles with smaller size than the resolution of NIR camera through analysis of mixed spectra with different kinds of algorithms.

2 Material and methodology

The test rig used in this investigation was the NIR sensor-based sorting system at the Department of Processing and Recycling (I.A.R.), RWTH Aachen University. A simplified scheme of the test rig is shown in figure 7.1.

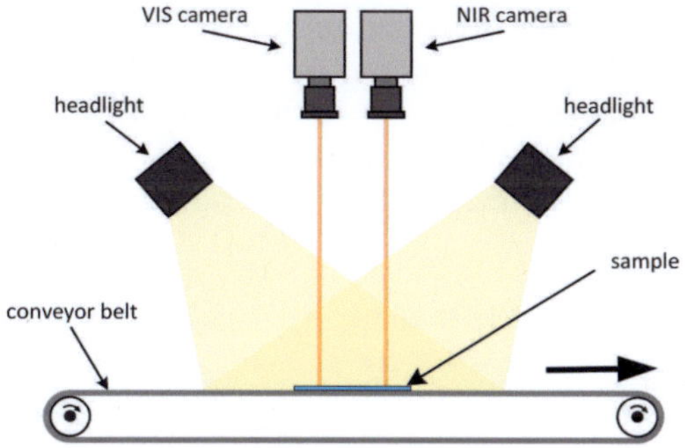

Figure 7.1: scheme of the test rig at I.A.R.

During the capturing process, the samples passed through the NIR light and the cameras simultaneously on a conveyer belt. The halogen lamps were placed with an angle to the capturing area of the two cameras to ensure enough light for the process. The conveyer belt of this test rig is made of black PVC, which reflects much less light comparing to other colors. The NIR-camera used was the model N17E from Specim®, Spectral Imaging Ltd, with a frame rate up to 30 fps. It captures the reflection of the light in the wavelength area between 900 nm and 1700 nm. As the capturing of the wavelength area between 900 – 1000 nm was not stable, only the wavelength area of 1000 – 1700 nm was analyzed in this study. The spatial resolution was 320 pixels in the capturing width with 400 mm and the spectral resolution was approximately 5 nm. In case of the VIS camera, the manufacturer is IDS Imaging Development Systems GmbH. The camera has a spatial resolution of 1280 pixels in the capturing width. The frame rate is up to 1550 fps as line camera with an automated optical inspection height of 4. Both NIR and VIS camera are applied as line camera. For the VIS camera, the line-photos are merged together as a two-dimensional (2D) picture. The NIR camera, however, provides each line a 2D picture, in which one direction is the spatial resolution of 320 pixels and the other direction with 256 pixels is the spectral resolution. The reflectance is reflected from the picture with different grey scales of each pixel. In the following, the grey scales are shown as a line in diagram to be intuitive.

As the frame rate of VIS camera is more than 50 times higher, and the spatial resolution 4 times higher than of NIR camera, a definition of the contact zones of NIR picture was achieved with the help of VIS camera. To clearly define the contact zones of the materials, the pictures of NIR and VIS camera were combined. The capturing with NIR camera was firstly merged to a picture to show the position and the size of the samples.

2.1 Algorithms

Different kinds of algorithms are tested for the identification of the mixed spectra. The most important character to determine the performance of the algorithms in prediction is the accuracy of the classification. Besides, the computation time was compared, since the results of the classification are often needed immediately.

Manual classification

There are different studies in which various manual classification algorithms for plastics detection with NIR spectra were developed [1,5]. The idea is to classify the materials according to the position and/or ratio of the spectra peaks. The spectra can be raw spectra or the spectra processed with first derivative. One of the examples is to distinguish among PET, Polypropylene (PP), Polystyrene (PS), High-Density-Polyethylene (HDPE) and Polyvinylchloride (PVC) through calculating the ratio of the reflectance in two different wavelength areas, 1656 and 1724 nm. The algorithm was capable to classify the materials according to the known ratio range of each plastic type, but was limited to the five types mentioned above [1]. The mixed spectra were firstly analyzed manually based on the classification algorithms developed. The reflectance of the contact zones with different compositions are shown and the characteristic peaks were found manually. The performance of the peaks, e.g., the position, the level and the ratio of positive and negative peaks were analyzed and the most relevant characteristic performances are chosen as classification factor for the mixed spectra.

Machine learning

Machine learning provides automated methods for data analysis to make computers modify or adapt their activities. In other words, with machine learning, the patterns in data are automatically detected and used to predict future data, for example, to classify the data [1, 3]. There are different types of machine learning and numerous algorithms within them. The algorithms which are tested in this investigation are decision trees, k Nearest Neighbors algorithm (KNN) and Support Vector Machines (SVM).

Decision tree Decision tree for classification has been more popular over recent years due to low computational cost. It is important for machine learning that the algorithm works as fast as possible since the results are often needed immediately for sorting or online quality control. The idea of classification tree is to start at the root of the tree and progress down to the leaves, until the features match and the decision is made. In other words, the classification is broken down into a set of logical disjunctions about each feature in turn. [5, 6] The constructing of decision tree algorithms is based on heuristics starting at the root and choosing the most informative feature at each step to construct the tree gradually [5, 6]. Firstly, the root is assigned a label according to a major vote among all labels over the training data. For a new node, a series of iteration is carried out and the effect of splitting a single leaf is examined on each iteration. The split which performs best among all possible splits is chosen to be a new node and local optimization is made at the construction of each node [6].

kNN Nearest Neighbor (NN) algorithms belong to the simplest of all machine learning algorithms for classification. The idea of kNN is to look at similar data and choose to be in the same class as them without searching for a predictor within some predicted class of functions. The training set is memorized, the label of any new instance is predicted on the basis of the labels of the closest neighbors in the training data. In other words, NN is a learning-by-memorization type of rule. [5,6]

The datapoints which positioned within input space are classified according to the nearest neighbors. K nearest neighbors could be identified and the class is set to the most common one out of those for the nearest neighbors. The choice of k is important. If k is too large, the consideration of points which are too far away reduces the accuracy. In case k is too small, the methods are sensitive to noise. Computing the distance to the datapoints in the training set is required for the algorithms, which can cost relatively much time. The computational costs are higher as the number of dimensions grows. [5]

SVM The SVM is one of the most popular and widely used algorithms in modern machine learning due to the computational advantages over probabilistic methods. It provides impressive classification performance on relatively large datasets. [5,6]

SVM algorithm was originally designed for learning linear predictors in high dimensional feature spaces for binary classification. The data are classified through searching for largest margin as large as possible. Figure 7.2 shows the principle of the SVM binary classification. The red and black lines are possible separators to classify the data and the separator in black should be chosen as separator due to largest margin. [6]

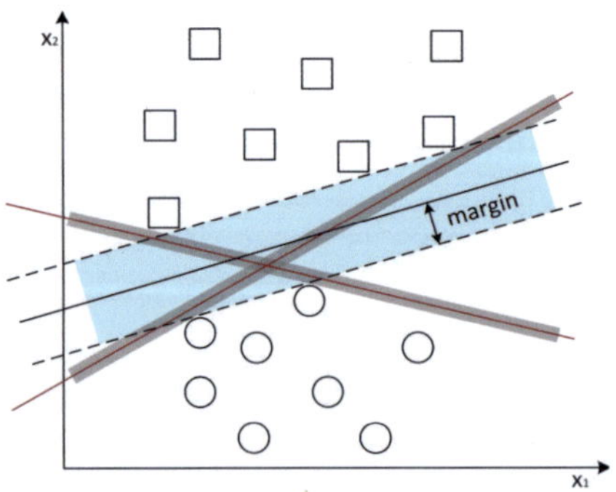

Figure 7.2: The principle of SVM binary classification.

The SVM is also capable to classify data which are not linearly separable. The solution is to introduce some slack variables so that the separator is a combination of various linear separators. Besides, SVM is not limited in two-class classification. For the problem of N-class classification, the SVM can be trained to learn how to classify one from all other classes, then a new SVM which classifies a new class from all others. This means, for N-class classification, there are N SVMs. [5]

2.2 Materials

For the analysis of mixed spectra, samples made from PP, HDPE, PS and PVC were collected. The materials were divided equally into two groups. The first group is for learning information. The mixed spectra of the first group were analyzed manually or learned with machine learning algorithms. The second group contributed to test the accuracy. For all the algorithms, the information for learning was the same and the data for testing purpose were identical.

3 Results and discussion

According to the known frame rate ratio and the resolution of both cameras, the relationship between the same pixels in NIR picture and in VIS picture could be confirmed. In the picture of VIS camera, the contact zones were chosen and the coordinates thereof were determined, the corresponding coordinates of the pixels in NIR picture can be accordingly calculated and clearly defined. The spectra data of the pixels are then analyzed.

3.1 Mixed spectra of plastics and background

For the analysis of the mixed spectra of PP, HDPE, PS and PVC with background, there are 9 classes for the classification: Background, pure PP, pure HDPE, pure PS, pure PVC, PP with background, HDPE with background, PS with background and PVC with background.

Manual classification

To analyze the data manually, the data for different classes were indicated in diagrams to find out the characters which are unique that could be used as classification factor. Figure 7.3 shows the raw spectra and the spectra process with the first derivative of learning pixels for PP, mixed pixels with PP mixed with background as well as background as examples. For the spectra processed with the first derivative, the thick lines are the average of all the values for each wavelength area.

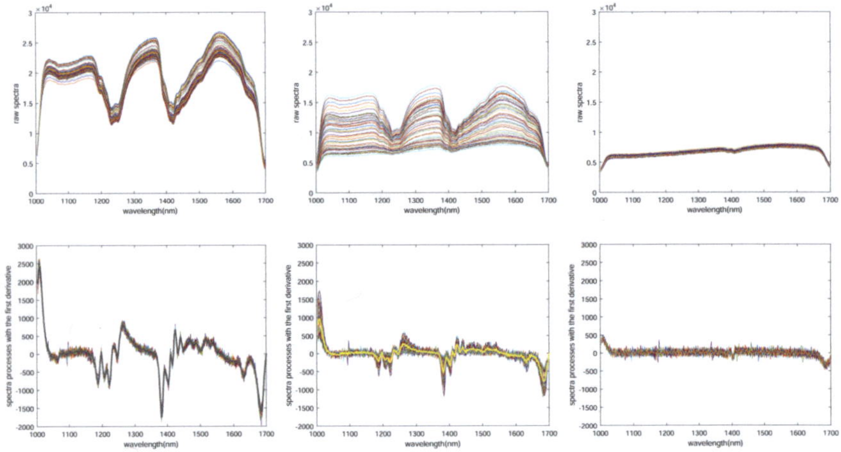

Figure 7.3: Raw spectra and first derivative for the manual analysis (from top left to bottom right: Raw spectra of PP, PP with background, background; first derivative of the same sequence).

According to the raw spectra, the differences between PP, background and PP with background were considerably big. The reflectance of PP was stronger than PP with background and the background reflects, as mentioned above, much less light. A general classification of PP, PP with background and background can be achieved with raw spectra values. However, in order to classify different kinds of mixed spectra, the classification with average values of reflectance is not sufficient. Moreover, the spectra have a large range in the reflectance of certain wavelength, see raw spectra of PP with background.

Since the form is characteristic for the classification, the spectra processed with first derivative were further analyzed and trained to classify the mixed spectra, along with the average value of raw spectra. The average value contributes to the classification between plastic, plastic with background and background, the first derivative is responsible for the classification of types of material. Looking at the first derivative of PP and PP with background, the peaks have the same positions, only the values are different. Thus, the values of the peaks are the classification factor between pure materials and the same type of material with background. Figure 7.4 shows the mixed spectra of PS with background, PVC with background as examples and the average values of all kinds of mixed spectra in one diagram.

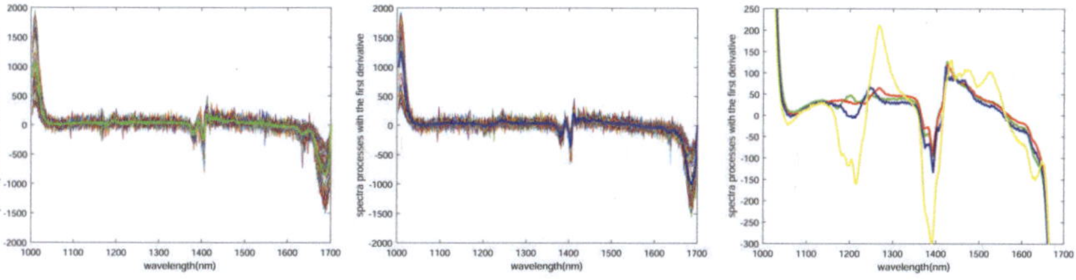

Figure 7.4: Mixed spectra processed with first derivative of PS with background, PVC with background and the average values (Red: HDPE with Background; Yellow: PP with background; Green: PS with background; Blue: PVC with background).

In the first two figures, the spectra are very similar to each other and it is difficult to classify the data. In the diagram at the right side, only the wavelength area from about 1050 to 1670 nm is shown to make the difference clearer. From the results, it can be seen that the distinct differences of HDPE with background, PS with background and PVC with background are in the wavelength area of approximately 1150 to 1300 nm. The characteristic peaks in this area are located in different wavelength, some of which are positive peaks and some are negative. Based on the information above, the algorithm for manual classification is defined as following:

- Pre-classification of the background: find the background with the average values of reflectance using a relatively low threshold, as the average value of some of the pixels with mixed spectra are similar to the value of background.

- Find the important peaks of the spectra processed with first derivative for each material, background included, and classify the pixels in the same class if they have the similar peaks
- According to the average values of the raw spectra and the values of peaks, the pixels are classified to pure material or material with background

The classification results of 4 samples with different materials as examples are shown in figure 7.5. The samples in the picture are HDPE, PP, PS, PVC from left to right. The colors which represent the mixed spectra of the materials are the same as the thick lines in figure 7.3, the black represent the background. The greyscales from low to high are HDPE, PP, PS, PVC.

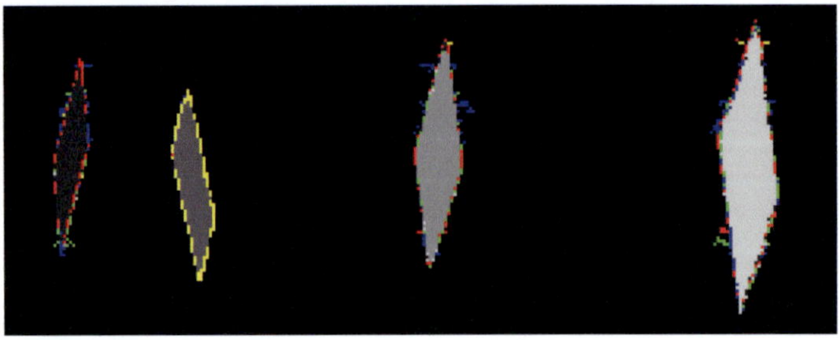

Figure 7.5: Classification results with manual classification.

As a result, the classification worked properly for most of the pixels for pure material. For the classification of mixed spectra, only pixels of PP with background were correctly classified. The accuracy for classifying other mixed spectra was low. In some cases, the background pixels were classified as mixed materials. The accuracy of the classification was about 90.7 % and the computational time of the classification was 5.18 seconds.

Decision tree

The information used for the analysis of the manual classification was learned with decision tree algorithms. Figure 7.6 demonstrates the best classification resulted from decision tree.

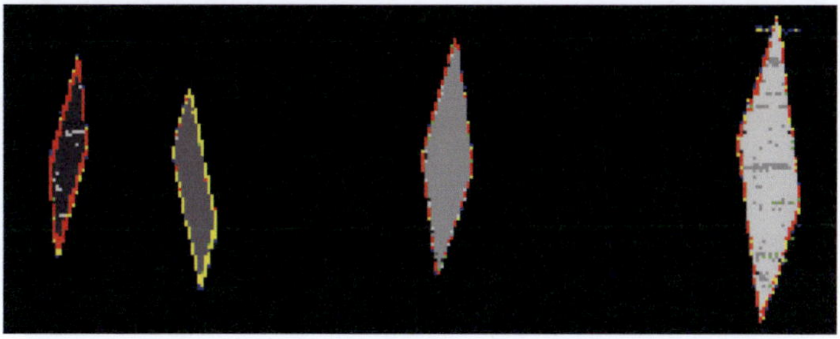

Figure 7.6: Classification results with decision tree algorithm.

With decision tree algorithm, the mixed spectra of HDPE with background, PP with background could be mostly classified to the right group, as well as pure PP and PS. The classification of pure HDPE and PVC was not very successful, as some of the pixels were classified as PS. The accuracy of classification for mixed spectra of PS with background was lower comparing to HDPE and PP with background. Almost all the mixed spectra of PVC with background were not classified correctly. The accuracy for training and classification was 91.5 % and the computational time was 2.85 seconds.

kNN

Figure 7.7 shows the classification results with kNN algorithm.

With kNN algorithm, almost all pixels of pure HDPE, PP and PS were classified properly. The accuracy of the classification of PVC was lower than the others, similar to the decision tree algorithm, a part of the pixels were classified as HDPE. For the classification of the mixed spectra, the accuracy decreased, since for HDPE with background and PP with background, some of the pixels were classified as background.

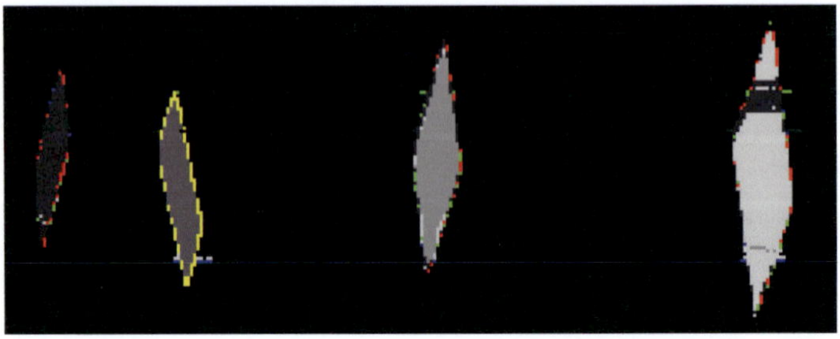

Figure 7.7: Classification results with kNN algorithm.

The classification of PS with background and PVC with background was not successful, only few pixels were right classified. The accuracy for training and classification was 89.4 % with a computational time of 17.4 seconds.

SVM

Figure 7.8 shows the best classification achieved of all the SVM algorithms.

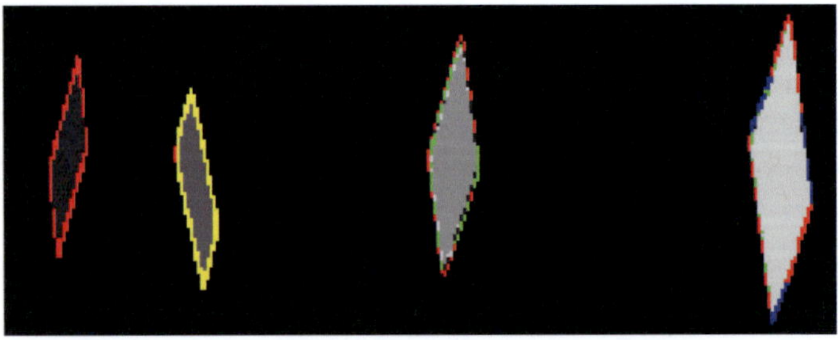

Figure 7.8: Classification results with SVM algorithm.

With this algorithm, the classification of both the pure material and mixed spectra was successful, comparing to other algorithms. However, the accuracy of classification of PS with background and PVC with background was lower than of other classes. The accuracy for the classification was 96.1 % with a computational time of 27.1 seconds.

The results of the classification with all kinds of algorithms show that the classification of mixed spectra of PS with background and PVC with background was more difficult than other classes. The reason for this is that the mixed spectra of HDPE with background, PS with background and PVC with background are very similar, like figure 7.4 shows. It must be noticed that most of the wrong classification was PS with background and PVC with background as HDPE with background, due to more data of mixed spectra of HDPE with background than the other two in the learning data. The pixels for the classification were more likely to be classified into the class with more data. Another reason why the classification accuracy is not high enough is the small size of the database. There were enough spectra for the learning of pure materials, for the mixed spectra, however, much less. A larger size of database brings, in the other side, a problem of increased computational time, especially for the kNN-Algorithms, as the distance to the datapoints must be calculated and compared.

3.2 Mixed spectra of different compositions of plastics

As the conveyer belt of the test rig was also plastic, the analysis of the mixed spectra of plastics with background is a special case of the analysis of different kinds of compositions. In that case, one of the components was certain, the conveyer belt. In order to classify the mixed spectra of the contact zones and the pure materials, there are 11 classes: Background, HDPE, PP, PS, PVC, HDPE with PP, HDPE with PS, HDPE with PVC, PP with PS, PP with PVC, PS with PVC. The analysis methods were the same as for the analysis of plastics with background. The classification results are shown below in table 7.1.

Table 7.1: Accuracy and computational time for the analysis of mixed spectra of different plastic compositions.

Algorithms	manual	Decision Tree	kNN	SVM
Accuracy (%)	89.3	91.0	92.5	96.5
Computational time (seconds)	9.8	10.4	28.7	48.8

The classification results show that the accuracy with SVM algorithm was higher than others, like the analysis of plastics with background.

However, the computation costed significantly more time. It must be mentioned that the accuracy and the computational cost are dependent on the size of learning information and the pixels chosen as learning information. In this case, the analysis and classification of 6 samples in one process results in a higher computational cost. One of the solutions to reduce the computational time of SVM is to analyze based on lines instead of objects. The classification can be more than 300 times faster, since the computational time listed above is for over 300 lines.

4 Conclusions

The analysis of mixed spectra of different kinds of plastics with black PVC as background, as well as of different kinds of compositions have been implemented. The classification of each of them was achieved through manual classification, decision tree algorithms, kNN algorithms and SVM algorithms. The results demonstrate that the classification of mixed spectra is generally possible and, the accuracy together with the computational time are depending on the used algorithms. For the classification of the mixed spectra of plastics with background and composition of plastics, the SVM algorithms proved to be the more accurate one, although the computation costs more time than the other algorithms. Classification manually is possible for pure materials, but it does not work properly for the mixed spectra. However, it must be mentioned that for the algorithms for manual classification, the way of programming is for each person different and the accuracy and computational time are depending on the program. In general, machine leaning algorithms are more universal, as the only effort is to pre-processing of learning information as input for the computer, the classification can be done automatically. This is easier for especially numerous types of materials, the data can be added and learned faster than manual analysis, since for manual analysis, data of all types of material must be compared.

With the successful analysis of mixed spectra of plastics and background, it is possible to detect and classify particles which are smaller than the resolution of NIR camera with NIR technology. Besides, the success of classification of mixed spectra of different compositions makes the detection and classification of heterogeneous material theoretically possible, which offers an additional option for plastic sorting.

References

1. S. M. Safavi and Z. Khani, "Identification and classification of plastic resins using near infrared reflectance p spectroscopy," 2012.
2. T. Pretz and J. Julius, "Stand der technik und entwicklung bei der berührungslosen sortierung von abfällen," *Österreichische Wasser- und Abfallwirtschaft*, vol. 60, no. 7, pp. 105–112, Aug 2008.
3. I. 4R Sustainability, "Demingling the mix: An assessment of commercially available automated sorting technology," 2011.
4. K. Nienhaus, Ed., *Sensor technologies : impulses for the raw materials industry*, ser. Schriftenreihe Zur Aufbereitung und Veredlung ; Bd. 50. Aachen: Shaker Verl., 2014. [Online]. Available: http://d-nb.info/1046907050/04
5. S. Marsland, *Machine learning : an algorithmic perspective*, 2nd ed., ser. Chapman and Hall/CRC machine learning and pattern recognition series. Boca Raton[u.a.]: CRC Press, 2015, erscheinungsjahr in Vorlageform:c 2015.
6. S. Shalev-Shwartz and S. Ben-David, *Understanding Machine Learning: From Theory to Algorithms*. Cambridge University Press, 2014.

Subpixel detection of peanut particles in wheat flour using near infrared hyperspectral imaging

Antoine Laborde[1], Benoit Jaillais[2], Anthony Boulanger[1], Delphine Jouan-Rimbaud Bouveresse[3], and Christophe B.Y. Cordella[3]

[1] GreenTropism,
75116 Paris, France
[2] StatSC INRA/ONIRIS,
44322 Nantes, France,
[3] UMR914 PNCA AgroParisTech,
75231 Paris, France

Abstract Hyperspectral imaging in near-infrared region (NIR) is a powerful tool for characterization and detection in food industry. In particular, the scan of powders is a subject of interest for adulteration evaluation. However, such samples involve intimate mixture hence complex non linear effect in the reflectance signal. In this study, Adaptive Matched Subspace Detector (AMSD) is implemented for detecting peanut flour adulteration in wheat flour. The method consists of a hypothesis test based on the linear mixing model. This is compared with a non supervised technique based on Principal Component Analysis rejection method. Results show that AMSD performs the best by detecting adulterated pixels in samples with global concentration from 20% down to 0.02%. A coefficient of determination of 0.90 is obtained between the number of detected pixels and the global concentration of samples. PCA rejection method shows relevant but insufficient results by detecting much fewer adulterated pixels than AMSD. This study shows that the implementation of AMSD is successful and more efficient than rejection method based on the inner product variability.

Keywords: Subpixel detection, peanut, hyperspectral.

1 Introduction

Near-infrared hyperspectral imaging (HSI) is a technique that provides both spatial and spectral information for a sample. The near-infrared range is a particularly interesting since no sample preparation is required and various organic information can be studied. Thanks to this, HSI has been recognized as an emerging tool for controlling food safety for a decade [1] . For example, HSI has been successfully employed to detect melamine adulteration in milk powder [2] [3] [4]. Melamine and milk particles were detected in the case of an intimate mixing and for pixel size bigger than particles. In this context, the resulting spectral signatures of the mixture is nonlinear and complex to explain [5]. However, since melamine and milk powder spectral signatures are very different, they can be directly used for the implementation of a detection method. This is done using Principal Component Analysis (PCA) [3], Partial Least Square Regression (PLSR) [4] or by spectral similarity analysis [2].

As the allergic population seems to grow, allergens contamination is a hot topic for food issue as well. Peanut adulteration in wheat flour has been achieved using HSI and PCA [6] . In this case, peanut particles were bigger than the pixel so that no intimate mixing occurs in the powder. However, the detection of peanut in wheat flour is more difficult since spectral signatures are closer than the melamine and milk situation.

Subpixel detection is a subject of interest in remote sensing application. For Earth observation, pixel field of view are about several meters so that each pixel may contain spectral contributions of several end members. As long as the mixing only occurs in the sensor, linear mixing model theoretically holds. However, for multi-layer samples or intimate mixing structure, the linear assumption is not valid. On the other hand, nonlinear models require a deep knowledge about the samples that are very difficult to obtain [5]. As a consequence, linear mixing model is often employed using additional interaction terms. The Adaptive Matched Subspace Detector (AMSD) is derived from the linear mixing model (LMM) using a hypothesis test. This detector is used at the subpixel context since each pixel is treated individually without spatial information [7].

In this study, we propose to address the detection of peanut particles in wheat flour at the subpixel level. AMSD technique is compared with a PCA model based rejection method to detected adulterated pixels of flour mixing.

2 Theory

2.1 AMSD

The LMM describes each pixel of a hyperspectral image as a linear combination of component spectra or endmembers (cf. equation 8.1).

$$x = \sum_{k=1}^{M} a_k s_k + w \tag{8.1}$$

where

x is the spectrum of the pixel;
s_k are the spectra of the M endmembers;
a_k are the abundances of the M endmembers;
M is the number of endmembers;
w is a vector that accounts for the lack-of-fit of the LMM.

In the LMM, the subspace S generated by the s_k vectors should be representative of all the chemical species in the mixing. For a detection problem, S is divided in two parts : the background subspace S_b and the target subspace S_t. The matrix S_b contains the spectra of the endmembers considered as background and S_t contains the targeted endmembers.

For the AMSD, the detection problem is a hypothesis test. In each case, a LMM is assumed according to the presence of the target. For the null hypothesis, the spectrum of the pixel is assumed to lie in the background subspace. The alternative hypothesis assumes x lies in the union of both subspaces S_t and S_b (cf. 8.2).

$$\begin{aligned} H_0 &: x = S_b a_b + w \\ H_1 &: x = S_t a_t + S_b a_b + w \end{aligned} \tag{8.2}$$

where we assume $w \hookrightarrow \mathcal{N}(0, \sigma_w^2 I)$.

Designing a detector for the hypothesis test can be done using the likelihood ratio (LR). Since the abundance vectors a_t and a_b as well as the noise variance σ_w^2 are unknown, the generalized likelihood ratio is used [7]. As a result, the ratio between the error sum of squares (SSE) under each hypothesis is used as a detector (cf. 8.3).

$$d_{AMSD}(x) = \frac{SSE_{H_0}}{SSE_{H_1}} - 1 \tag{8.3}$$

where

$$SSE_{H_0} = (x - S_b a_b)^T (x - S_b a_b),$$
$$SSE_{H_1} = (x - S_t a_t + S_b a_b)^T (x - S_t a_t + S_b a_b).$$

2.2 PCA rejection method

In this study, PCA provides orthogonal components for modeling wheat pure sample: V_b. Only the k first components are kept to retain the main spectral variance: V_{b_k}. As a result, an orthogonal projector can be constructed (cf. 8.4).

$$P_{b_k}^{\perp} = 1 - V_{b_k}^T V_{b_k} \tag{8.4}$$

Using the projector $P_{b_k}^{\perp}$, the residual of each pixel with respect to the PCA model based on the pure wheat sample can be computed. Finally, the sum of squares (SS) of these residuals are used as a metric for the pixel rejection method (cf. 8.5).

$$d_{rejection}(x) = SS(x P_{b_k}^{\perp}) \tag{8.5}$$

3 Material and methods

3.1 Samples

Defatted peanut flour and white wheat flour were bought and mixed together in different proportions. A total of 8 weight concentrations of peanut were obtained: 20%, 10%, 5%, 2%, 1%, 0.5% 0.2% and 0.02%.

For each concentration, 3 replicates of approximately 13 g of flour were measured as well as one pure peanut flour sample and one pure wheat flour sample. Each sample was prepared using a precision balance (accuracy of 0.01g) and by manually shaking the resulting mix. Samples were put into a polylactic (PLA) sample holder of 7 mm depth for the hyperspectral measurement.

3.2 Hyperspectral acquisition

A SWIR camera from SPECIM (SPECIM, Spectral Imaging Ltd., Oulu, Finland) was used for hyperspectral measurement. The samples were lightened by four halogen lamps at 58cm from the camera. Black measurement and white reference were acquired in order to obtained the normalized reflectance.

3.3 Detector design

For designing the AMSD, non negative matrix factorization (NMF) was applied on the pure wheat flour and peanut flour sample. The k first components were used to design the matrix S_b and S_t. When the detector is applied on a test image, a non negative least square resolution is applied on each pixel to calculate the corresponding abundance vectors a_t and a_b. Then, the estimation of x under each hypothesis is used for the calculation of SSE_{H_0} and SSE_{H_1}. The resulting value of $d_{AMSD}(x)$ must be finally compared to a threshold value η which is obtained according to equation 8.6. This boils down to minimizing the probability of false alarm on the test images.

$$\eta = \max_{x \in X_0} d_{AMSD}(x) \tag{8.6}$$

where X_0 is the matrix containing the spectra from the reference pure wheat flour image.

Similarly, the PCA rejection method gives a final detection by thresholding $d_{rejection}(x)$. The threshold value is obtained from 8.6 by replacing $d_{AMSD}(x)$ with $d_{rejection}(x)$.

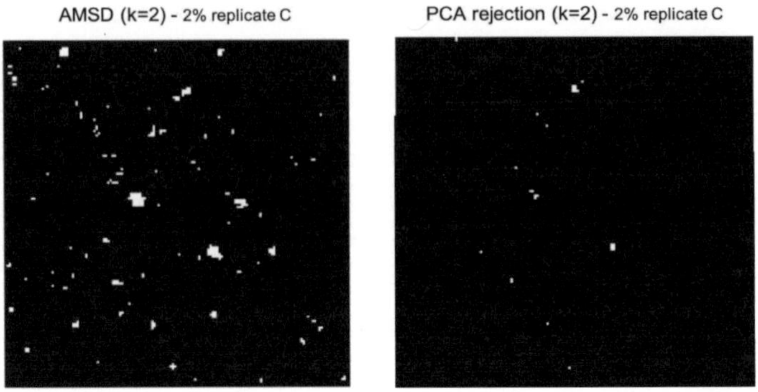

Figure 8.1: Detection map for wheat flour mixed with 2% of peanut flour (replicate C) using the AMSD (left) and the PCA rejection method (right). White pixels: detection, black pixels: no detection.

4 Results and discussion

Even though the two methods are very different, they both provide consistent results. Figure 8.1 illustrates the fact that the detection maps obtained on a same sample show similar spatial results. Indeed, even if the PCA rejection method detects much fewer pixels than AMSD does, the position of the detected pixels correspond to detected clusters on the AMSD detection map.

Table 8.1 exhibits a high correlation between the number of detected pixels and the expected concentration of peanut for the AMSD method. Results also show that AMSD is robust to the choice of k. On the other side, the PCA rejection method exhibits lower R^2 score as well as a high dependency to the value of k.

These results are explained by the fact that the PCA rejection method generally detects much fewer pixels than AMSD. This can be seen as an example on Figure 8.1. Indeed, in most cases, PCA rejection works well for location where clusters of peanut particle are present. In this case, there is more chance that a pixel has an almost full contribution of peanut. More generally, PCA rejection method has the advantage to not be dedicated to one adulterant spectral signature. In return, the detection method is less sensitive to the peanut adulteration. Adding more than 2 components to the rejection model (choosing $k > 2$) makes R^2 worst. This is because the accepted variability increases so that peanut particles are comprised in it and thus, not detected.

For the subpixel detection problem, the contribution of the target may be hidden by the background. If their spectral signatures are similar, the detection may be difficult. In this case, supervised target detection is necessary. Indeed, the change in the spectral signal may be of the same order than the background variability which makes unsupervised method fail.

Table 8.1: Coefficient of determination (R^2) between the number of detected pixels in each image and the corresponding concentration of peanut flour.

k	1	2	3
$R^2 AMSD$	0.90	0.90	0.89
$R^2 PCA$	0.55	0.61	0.19

5 Conclusion

The study shows the AMSD approach is relevant for subpixel detection problem. Even if the complexity of the mix may involve non linear effects on the signal mixture, the hypothesis test based linear mixing models is relevant. In contrast, the PCA rejection method gives interesting results but appears to be insufficient to detect the majority of the adulterated pixels. Indeed, in this model, outliers are assumed to have higher spectral differences than the inner product variability. In the case of peanut and wheat flour, this assumption appears to be questionable. Finally, AMSD enables to find adulterated pixels down to a global concentration of 0.02% but the detector sensitivity at the pixel level is still to be investigated. The high R^2 score obtained between the number of detected pixels and the true sample concentration shows that AMSD provide a successful and relevant detection of peanut in wheat at the subpixel level.

References

1. A. Gowen, C. O'Donnell, P. Cullen, D. G., and J. Frias, "Hyperspectral imaging an emerging process analytical tool for food quality and safety control," *Trends in Food Science and Technology*, vol. 18, pp. 590–598, 2007.

2. X. Fu, M. S. Kim, K. Chao, J. Qin, J. Lim, L. H., A. Garrido-Varo, P.-M. D., and Y. Ying, "Detection of melamine in milk powders based on nir hyperspectral imaging and spectral similarity analyses," *Journal of Food Engineering*, vol. 124, pp. 97–104, 2014.

3. J. A. Fernandez Pierna, D. Vincke, P. Dardenne, Z. Yang, L. Han, and B. V., "Line scan hyperspectral imaging spectroscopy for the early detection of melamine and cyanuric acid in feed," *Journal of Near Infrared Spectroscopy*, vol. 22, pp. 103–112, June 2014.

4. J. Lim, G. Kim, C. Mo, M. S. Kim, K. Chao, J. Qin, X. Fu, I. Baek, and B. Cho, "Detection of melamine in milk powders using near-infrared hyperspectral imaging combined with regression coefficient of partial least square regression model," *Talanta*, vol. 151, pp. 183–191, 2016.

5. J. M. Bioucas-Dias, A. Plaza, N. Dobigeon, M. Parente, Q. Du, P. Gader, and J. Chanussot, "Hyperspectral unmixing overview: Geometrical, statistical, and sparse regression-based approaches," *IEEE Journal of Selected Topics in Applied Earth Observations and Remote Sensing*, vol. 5, no. 2, pp. 354–379, 2012.

6. P. Mishra, P. Herrero-Langreo, A.and Barreiro, J. Roger, B. Diezma, N. Gorretta, and L. Lleo, "Detection and quantification of peanut traces in wheat flour by near infrared hyperspectral imaging spectroscopy using principal-component analysis," *Journal of Near Infrared Spectroscopy*, vol. 23, pp. 15–22, February 2015.

7. D. Manolakis, C. Siracusa, and S. G., "Hyperspectral subpixel target detection using the linear mixing model," *IEEE Transactions on Geoscience and Remote Sensing*, vol. 39, no. 7, pp. 1392–1409, July 2001.

Automatic visual inspection based on trajectory data

Georg Maier, Nico Mürdter, Robin Gruna,
Thomas Längle, and Jürgen Beyerer

Fraunhofer Institute of Optronics, System Technologies
and Image Exploitation IOSB
Fraunhoferstr. 1, 76131 Karlsruhe, Germany

Abstract Automatic inspection tasks have successfully been implemented in several industrial fields and are of growing importance. Visual inspection using optical sensors is wide spread due to the vast variety of different sensors, observable features and comparatively low prices. It seems obvious that corresponding systems are blind towards mechanical features and inspection of those typically requires highly specialized, inflexible and costly systems. Recently, we have shown in the context of sensor-based sorting that tracking objects over a time period allows deriving motion-based features which potentially enable discrimination of optically identical objects, although an optical sensor is used. In this paper, we take one step back from the specific application and study the classification of test objects based on their trajectories. The objects are observed while receiving a certain impulse. We further refrain from manually designing features but use raw coordinates as extracted from a series of images. The success of the method is demonstrated by discriminating spheres made of similar plastic types while bouncing off a plane.

Keywords: Machine vision, motion features, tracking.

1 Introduction

How can a cooked egg be distinguished from a raw one? Obviously, the difference cannot be determined by their appearance. A common household trick is to lay both eggs on a flat surface, rotate them like a spinning top and observe their rotation. While the boiled egg rotates uniformly, the raw egg performs a much more unstable movement due to the inertia of the liquid interior of the egg. This example demonstrates how an object to be tested is stimulated within the framework of an experiment in order to observe a characteristic behaviour. Due to their cognitive abilities, humans are immediately able to evaluate the observed movement behaviour and distinguish between the two objects. To a certain extent, an optical inspection is carried out here on the basis of a non-optical object property, namely the inertial tensor.

Away from the home kitchen, the task of sorting particles contained in a material stream according to certain criteria exists in several industrial fields. There exist two main types of systems for automation of the sorting process, namely mechanical sorting and sensor-based sorting [1]. Examples of mechanical sorting include sieving for separation based on size, sink–float processes for separating materials based on specific gravity and air-stream separation for separating particles with different aerodynamic characteristics. In sensor-based sorting, the characteristic used to distinguish particles from different classes determines the choice of the sensor used. For instance, RGB cameras are used for discrimination based on color, texture and shape, hyperspectral cameras can be used to retrieve information about the chemical composition of the particles and X-ray in order to measure the atomic density.

1.1 Problem statement and contribution

In the introductory example, we were interested in sorting objects according to mechanical properties. For many cases, this can be achieved by using mechanical sorting as discussed above. However, such processes typically suffer from a lack of flexibility, limited throughput and/or cost-intensive implementation. Sensor-based sorting systems appear to be an attractive alternative in all these regards. However, systems designed for high-throughput typically use imaging sensors and are hence by definition limited to optically perceivable characteristics.

In this paper, we propose a machine vision approach for the classification of objects based on non-optical properties in the context of automatic visual inspection. Our approach is based on the use of an area-scan camera in combination with object tracking methods. The classification is based on the trajectories of objects as observed in a specific scene. The movement of the objects is tracked using an image sequence recorded at a high temporal resolution. We present an experimental setup in which the objects are observed while receiving a certain impulse. The setup supports the generation of huge datasets by realizing a circulation of test objects. With the help of machine learning, it is shown that optically identical objects made of similar materials can be distinguished from each other based on their trajectories without any further feature engineering. The proposed approach can easily be extended for high throughput applications and requires inexpensive hardware.

1.2 Related work

Although the use of imaging sensors dominates in sensor-based sorting, other systems have been proposed to sort materials on the basis of non-optical properties. An example is performing classification based on impact resonant acoustic emissions. For instance, in [2], the applicability of such sorting systems is evaluated for the detection of damaged wheat kernels, including defects that are optically not perceivable. In [3], the authors propose a similar system for the sorting of End-of-Life vehicles' plastic materials. Their system further includes laser triangulation scanning to combine information regarding the size of single plastic flakes with features derived from the impact acoustic.

Several works have also discussed the idea of performing classification or quality assessment on the basis of motion information obtained from image data. For instance, in [4], two material properties of fabric, namely stiffness and area weight, are estimated based on motion induced by unknown wind forces. The authors propose a framework which includes extraction of the magnitudes of motion from video data, deriving statistical features and implements a regression model to estimate the material properties. In [5] a quality control system for application in an industrial setting based on the tracking of sputters during a laser-welding process is proposed. The events are tracked at a high frame rate in order to distinguish strong sputter events that are critical to the welding process from harmless ones. Regression of physical properties of objects from video data has also recently been studied. Motivated by gaining knowledge about how humans learn to predict motion of objects in the real world, the authors propose a model that allows predicting physical properties which are then fed into a physics engine in order to simulate the continuation of a dynamic scene [6].

Recently, we have proposed utilizing motion-based features for the characterization of materials in sensor-based sorting [7, 8]. We have shown that spheres made of different materials can be distinguished based on their motion while being transported on a conveyor belt. However, to that point, we restricted ourselves to using test objects made of strongly differing materials. Furthermore, rather primitive, hand-crafted features based on motion statistics were used and only passively induced interaction with the environment, in this case friction with the conveyor belt, was considered. The study presented here distinguishes itself from the former one in that very similar materials are used as test objects, no feature engineering is performed and an active impulse on the test objects is observed.

2 Materials and methods

The following is a description of the setup designed to acquire a dataset and the methods used for analyzing the data.

2.1 Data acquisition

The phenomenon we want to observe in our experimental setup is elastic collision. We adopt the setup from [3] by using an inclined plane to accelerate the test objects and a second plane with which the objects collide, see Figure 9.1. Hence, we observe the test objects while bouncing off the second plane. After the collision(s), the test objects fall into a funnel and are re-applied on the inclined plane by using a Venturi loader.

With respect to the optical hardware, we use the camera Ximea xiQ MQ022 and an 8 mm lens. The camera is connected to a computer using the USB 3.0 interface. We further crop the image to an resolution of 1220×950 pixels and record images at 194 fps. Illumination is realized by using an LED back light.

As for test objects, we are interested in using objects of the same shape made of different, yet similar materials. For this purpose, we created 3D prints of sphere shaped test objects made of different plastics.

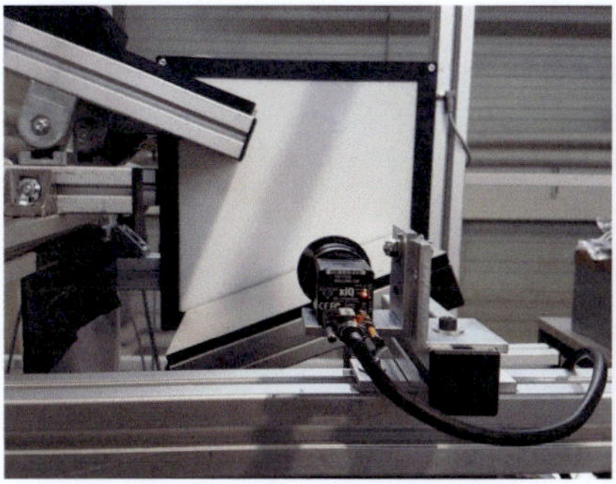

(a) Field of view of the camera.

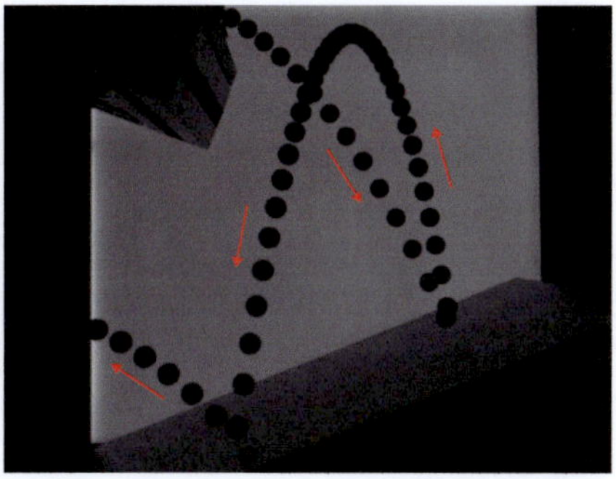

(b) Exemplary motion pattern observed by the camera.

Figure 9.1: Impressions of the observed experimental situation.

We consider 8 materials from 4 different types of plastic, namely acrylonitrile butadiene styrene (ABS), polyamide (PA), polycarbonates (PC) and polypropylen (PP). All spheres have a diameter of 10 mm. An impression of the test objects is provided in Figure 9.2. It is important to note that the difference in appearance, i.e., color, is not used for the classification.

Figure 9.2: Photo of the test objects, from l. t. r.: ABS1, ABS2, PA1, PA2, PC1, PC2, PP1, PP2.

Our goal is to extract discrete time series data from the images which represent the path traveled by the test objects in 2D space. We neglect the third dimension as the objects move approximately only in one plane and the camera points perpendicular to that plane. In order to locate an object in an image, we apply image processing. In a first step, an image received from the camera is segmented using background subtraction using the implementation from the OpenCV library which is based on [9, 10]. The resulting binary image is further pre-processed using morphological operations, namely erosion and subsequent dilation, followed by Gaussian filtering. In case an object is contained in the image, its contour is extracted using the implementation of [11] in OpenCV, yielding a measurement of form

$$p(t) := (x, y, t)\ . \tag{9.1}$$

The contextual attribute of the time series is a timestamp and the behavioural attribute is given by the 2D position of the center of the sphere in the image. A trajectory is then modelled as a set of subsequent measurements:

$$T := \{p(t_1), \ldots, p(t_n) \mid t_n \leq t_{n+1}\}\ . \tag{9.2}$$

As has been mentioned, our experimental setup enables circulation of a test object by re-applying it over and over again. Therefore, we need to determine which measurements belong to a single trajectory and which to different ones. We can group measurements to a single trajectory by determining the time difference between two measurements. At a constant recording speed, a trajectory is only valid if two consecutive points also originate from two directly consecutive images of the recording. A trajectory of a single pass can hence be formalized as

$$T := \{p(t_1), \ldots, p(t_n) \mid t_n < t_{n+1}, t_{n+1} - t_n \leq \epsilon\} \tag{9.3}$$

where $\epsilon := {}^{1}/_{\text{fps}}$ is the time between two consecutive frames.

2.2 Data preparation and analysis

Prior to data analysis, we perform data cleaning in order to make sure we only work with trajectories without missing or possibly faulty measurements. For instance, we require that for each time point only a single measurement exists. The movement of each object is therefore described by a trajectory consisting of a temporally unambiguous point set to ensure that no faulty detection is included. We further only consider complete trajectories. The latter is ensured by exploiting a priori knowledge about the scene. We require that the first measurement lies within the area were the test objects enter the scene, i.e., the upper left corner with respect to Figure 9.1, and the last measurement where the objects leave the scene, i.e, the lower left corner. Using the described procedure, we create a dataset containing individual trajectories that are labeled with the corresponding material. For each of the 8 materials, the resulting dataset contains more than 10000 trajectories that were deemed valid.

We intend to use the recorded coordinates directly as the input for the classification without any further feature extraction. However, the trajectories are of varying length which results in a variable length of the feature vector, which is not supported by many classification algorithms. Therefore, for our experiments, we use two ways to extract trajectories of fixed length. The first method is extraction and padding. We calculate the median length of all recorded trajectories and use this length to either crop trajectories that contain more measurements or pad shorter trajectories to the length by filling up with zero-valued coordinates. The second method is based on geometric interpolation of the trajectories. The sampling is calculated with the help of a spline interpolation and the trajectories are up-sampled to 256 data points. We further discard the temporal component, i.e., the timestamp associated with each measurement, for the interpolation.

As a learning model, we use a support vector machine (SVM) with a radial basis function (RBF) kernel. The features, i.e., the coordinates, are standardized by removing the mean and scaling to unit variance.

3 Experimental results

For the experimental validation, we consider two types of classification problems. The first problem is to classify the material based on the trajectory data according to the plastic type as described in Section 2.1. For each type, there exist two individual test objects. For the second classification problem each individual test object is to be classified. We use 10000 trajectories of each material for the training and testing, resulting in a total of 80000 samples. The dataset is split into train and test sets whereas the size of the test set is 30% of the entire dataset.

Results when using cropped and padded trajectories are provided in Figure 9.3. As can be seen from Figure 9.3 (a), test objects of type PA and PC can be distinguished very well from the other types while a noteworthy amount of false classifications happen for ABS and PP.

With respect to the latter, it can also be seen that the wrong classifications happen mainly between these two classes, i.e., ABS test objects are held falsely for PP and vice versa. From Figure 9.3 (b), the amount of false classifications with respect to the material within the plastic types can further be seen. It can be observed that with respect to PA, for instance, a large amount of false classification happen within the type, while this is not the case for PC. The false classifications happening between ABS and PP can be seen as well.

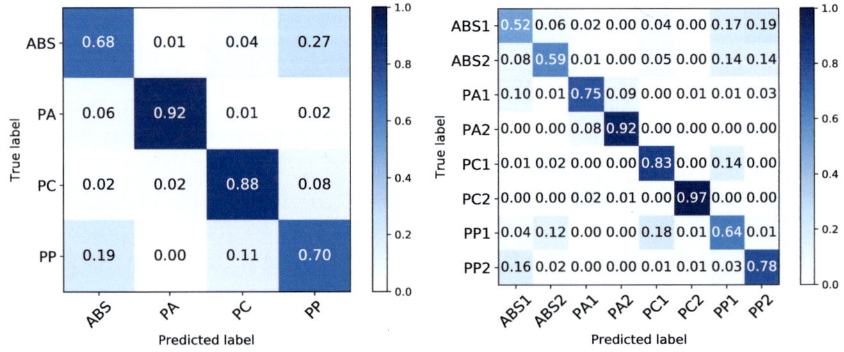

(a) Results using material types.

(b) Results using individual test objects.

Figure 9.3: Normalized confusion matrices for classification results for cropped and padded trajectories.

Results for the geometrically interpolated trajectories are very similar to those using the cropped and padded trajectories, see Figure 9.4. Overall, a slight loss in classification performance can be observed, which might be explained by the loss of temporal information. More precisely, the data does not allow to extract information whether a test object passes the experiment faster than another one. In turn, results show that the cropping and padding did not harm the classification performance, which suggests that the additional step of interpolation is not necessary.

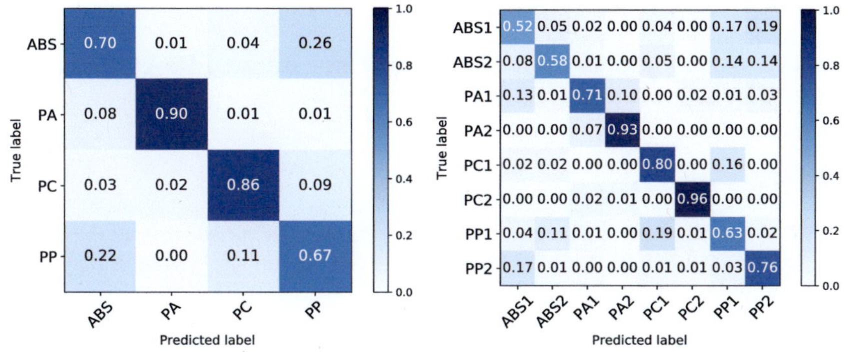

(a) Results using material types. (b) Results using individual test objects.

Figure 9.4: Normalized confusion matrices for classification results for geometrically interpolated trajectories.

4 Conclusions

In this paper, we have extended our previous work on motion-based classification for application in automatic visual inspection. We designed an experimental setup suitable for the recording of huge amounts of data which makes application of purely data driven learning models feasible. Furthermore, we showed that modelling the trajectory as a time series with a timestamp as the contextual and 2D position as behavioural attribute suffices to achieve high classification performance, making feature engineering dispensable.

In the near future, we intend to gain more knowledge about the robustness of the classification performance by not only mixing materials but also shapes of the test objects. Furthermore, we want to integrate the approach in sensor-based sorting by incrementally adapting the observed situation. For instance, instead of an impulse induced by a collision, a rippled chute could be used as a transport mechanism. Lastly, the approach can be made applicable for high throughput applications by integrating multiobject tracking. This would allow motion-based classification of several objects observed at the same time.

Acknowledgment

This work was supported by the Fraunhofer Internal Programs under Grant No. Discover 614 068.

References

1. S. P. Gundupalli, S. Hait, and A. Thakur, "A review on automated sorting of source-separated municipal solid waste for recycling," *Waste management*, vol. 60, pp. 56–74, 2017.
2. T. C. Pearson, A. E. Cetin, A. H. Tewfik, and R. P. Haff, "Feasibility of impact-acoustic emissions for detection of damaged wheat kernels," *Digital Signal Processing*, vol. 17, no. 3, pp. 617–633, 2007.
3. J. Huang, C. Tian, J. Ren, and Z. Bian, "Study on Impact Acoustic—Visual Sensor-Based Sorting of ELV Plastic Materials," *Sensors*, vol. 17, no. 6, p. 1325, 2017.
4. K. L. Bouman, B. Xiao, P. Battaglia, and W. T. Freeman, "Estimating the Material Properties of Fabric from Video," in *Computer Vision (ICCV), 2013 IEEE International Conference on*. IEEE, 2013, pp. 1984–1991.
5. M. Jager, S. Humbert, and F. A. Hamprecht, "Sputter Tracking for the Automatic Monitoring of Industrial Laser-Welding Processes," *IEEE Transactions on Industrial Electronics*, vol. 55, no. 5, pp. 2177–2184, May 2008.
6. J. Wu, I. Yildirim, J. J. Lim, B. Freeman, and J. Tenenbaum, "Galileo: Perceiving physical object properties by integrating a physics engine with deep learning," in *Advances in neural information processing systems*, 2015, pp. 127–135.
7. G. Maier, F. Pfaff, C. Pieper, R. Gruna, B. Noack, H. Kruggel-Emden, T. Längle, U. D. Hanebeck, S. Wirtz, and J. Scherer, Viktor Beyerer, "Improving material characterization in sensor-based sorting by utilizing motion information," in *OCM 2017 - Optical Characterization of Materials*. KIT Scientific Publishing, 2017.
8. G. Maier, F. Pfaff, F. Becker, C. Pieper, R. Gruna, B. Noack, H. Kruggel-Emden, T. Längle, U. D. Hanebeck, S. Wirtz *et al.*, "Motion-based material characterization in sensor-based sorting," *tm-Technisches Messen*, vol. 85, no. 3, pp. 202–210, 2018.
9. Z. Zivkovic, "Improved adaptive gaussian mixture model for background subtraction," in *Pattern Recognition, 2004. ICPR 2004. Proceedings of the 17th International Conference on*, vol. 2. IEEE, 2004, pp. 28–31.

10. Z. Zivkovic and F. Van Der Heijden, "Efficient adaptive density estimation per image pixel for the task of background subtraction," *Pattern recognition letters*, vol. 27, no. 7, pp. 773–780, 2006.

11. S. Suzuki *et al.*, "Topological structural analysis of digitized binary images by border following," *Computer vision, graphics, and image processing*, vol. 30, no. 1, pp. 32–46, 1985.

PhasmaFOOD - A miniaturized multi-sensor solution for rapid, non-destructive food quality assessment

Benedikt Groß[1], Susanne Hintschich[2], Milenko Tošić[3], Paraskevas Bourgos[4], Konstantinos Tsoumanis[4], and Francesca Romana Bertani[5]

[1] Freie Universität Berlin, Institut für Informatik
Heisenberg Communications and Information Theory Group
Takustraße 9, 14195 Berlin (Germany)
[2] Fraunhofer Institut für Photonische Mikrosysteme IPMS
Maria-Reiche-Str. 2, 01109 Dresden (Germany)
[3] Vizlore Labs Foundation
Braće Ribnikar 56, 21000 Novi Sad (Serbia)
[4] Wings ICT Solutions
189 Siggrou Avenue, 17121 Athens (Greece)
[5] CNR-IFN Institute for Photonics and Nanotechnologies
Via Cineto Romano 42, 00156 Rome (Italy)

Abstract PhasmaFOOD is a H2020 project with the goal of building a miniaturized, smart multi-sensor food scanner. Equipped with a NIR sensor, a UV-VIS sensor and a RGB camera it aims to be a portable, highly versatile solution for various food safety issues, ranging from aflatoxin detection in grains and nuts, over shelf-life prediction in meats and fish to detection of adulteration in meat, edible oils and alcoholic beverages. The unique combination of sensors, operation via a smartphone application and sophisticated data analysis methods offer the possibility of rapid, non-destructive measurements that can - in contrast to costly and slow laboratory instruments - be applied at every stage of the production chain, from farm to fork. After a brief introduction of the PhasmaFOOD system architecture the data analysis approach, especially the image analysis, based on dictionary learning is explained in detail.

Keywords: PhasmaFOOD, food scanner, optical sensing, spectroscopy, learning, image classification, image compression.

1 Introduction

PhasmaFOOD (www.phasmafood.eu) is a H2020 funded project of the European Union with a strong consortium of 9 stakeholders with expertise in food safety, spectroscopy, hardware and software development and machine learning, namely Intrasoft International S.A., Wings ICT Solutions, Ltd, VizLore Labs Foundation, RIKILT - Wageningen Reasearch, Agricultural University of Athens, Italian National Research Council, University of Rome Tor Vergata, Fraunhofer IPMS and Freie Universität Berlin. The objective of the PhasmaFOOD project is to develop a miniaturized, portable, smart multi-sensor food scanner. The system comprises a miniaturized, portable device integrating three different sensors and various light sources and a distributed software architecture. The PhasmaFOOD software architecture consists of a programmable micro-controller that steers the sensors in the portable device, a mobile app that serves as an interface to the user and is used to conduct measurements, calibrate the device and present recommendations based on the decision making in the cloud platform. The unique combination of three different optical sensors, a Near Infra-Red (NIR) spectrometer, a UltraViolet (UV) - Visible (VIS) spectrometer, operable in reflectance and fluorescence mode, a high resolution color imaging system, and sophisticated machine learning algorithms offer the potential to cover a wide range of applications in food safety.

The PhasmaFOOD solution is designed to meet three major requirements: **Portability**: the spectrometer is hand-held and can be configured on the mobile app. Hence, it works in various environments where food is sold or processed. **Versatility**: The specific combination of sensors (NIR spectrometer, UV-VIS spectrometer and CMOS camera) covers a spectal range from 400nm to 1900 nm, and, via the camera provides also textural information about the sample at hand. Hence, a wide range of food types and use cases can be targeted. **Fast, non-destructive predictions**: The three optical sensors work without the need to damage the product under investigation and deliver a measurement instantly. Therefore, it is well suited to time-critical problems like the shelf-life prediction of raw meat or fish, where waiting several days for results from laboratory measurements is not an option. The targeted use cases include:

1. Detection of mycotoxins in various grains and nuts. Aflatoxin detection.
2. Detection of (early signs of) spoilage in fruits, vegetables, meat and fish. Shelf-life prediction.
3. Detection of food fraud in alcoholic beverages, oil, milk powder and meat.

2 PhasmaFOOD system architecture

The PhasmaFOOD system consists of a miniaturized sensing device, a mobile application and the PhasmaFOOD cloud platform. The sensing device is used to take measurements of food samples with its integrated optical sensors. The sensing system is connected via bluetooth to a smart mobile device, such as a tablet or mobile phone, from which it is operated via the PhasmaFOOD mobile application. The mobile app receives data from the sensing device and forwards them to the cloud platform. On the PhasmaFOOD cloud platform the data is stored in the database and decision making algorithms are applied to incoming measurements. The predictions obtained from the use-case specific analysis algorithms are sent back to the mobile application and presented to the user.

2.1 Sensing device

The PhasmaFOOD sensing device is a portable multi-sensor device, comprising the sensing sub-unit, in which a NIR spectrometer, a UV-VIS spectrometer and a CMOS camera, illumination units and driving boards for all components are located, and the electronics sub-unit, a custom-built microcontroller, equipped with a recharchable battery, several communication interfaces (USB, BLE, WiFI), external memory (microSD) and additional sensors (inertial measurement unit, temperature sensor). The electronics sub-unit is able to configure the sensing sub-unit, read-in the raw sensor data, perform preprocessing operations and communicate with the mobile app. Due to the integration of an ARM processor, RAM and a FPGA unit even advanced processing of sensory data can be performed on the sensing device itself. The details of the electronics sub-unit can be found in [1] The sensing sub-unit (shown in figure 10.1(a))and the electronics sub-unit are mounted in a 3D-printed housing as shown in figure 10.1(b).

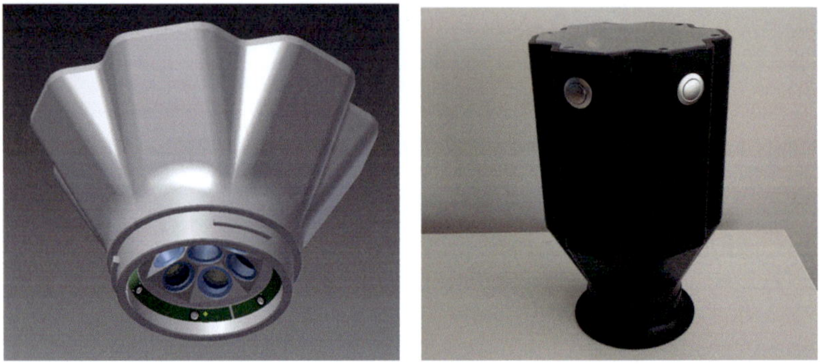

(a) PhasmaFOOD sensing sub-unit (b) PhasmaFOOD portable multi-sensor device

Special emphasis was given to a modular design in order to enable the replacement of sensing or lighting components. For the current prototype the following sensors were chosen: A miniaturized NIR spectrometer by Fraunhofer IPMS [2] (spectral range: $1000 - 1900nm$, size: $17 \times 12 \times 16mm^3$), the Hamamatsu C12880MA UV-VIS spectrometer (spectral range: $340 - 850nm$, size: $20.1 \times 12.5 \times 10.1mm^3$), and the Ximea MU9PC-MH CMOS camera (resolution: $5MP$, size: $15 \times 15 \times 8mm^3$). The range of the two spectrometers covers the entire visible and the near infra-red spectrum and is supported by a RGB camera to include spatial information as well. The sensors are accompanied by various lighting units, i.e. white LEDs, a NIR and a UV lightsource. Hence, the device is able to record a NIR spectrum, a fluorescence measurement, a visible reflectance spectrum of the sample under UV illumination and a RGB camera image.

2.2 Mobile application

The device is operated by the user via the PhasmaFOOD mobile app. In the mobile app the user selects one of the pre-defined use cases and the food type under consideration. The app then guides the user through the measurement process, displays the data and presents analysis results in comprehensible form. Expert users can also configure the sensing device for new use cases, adjust the lighting and tweak the parameters of the sensors, such as integration time, number of internal measurements etc. through the app. The measurements received from the device via BLE, together with additional input from the user are bundled in one json object and sent to the cloud platform for further processing and analysis. The current status of the mobile application is described in [3].

2.3 Cloud platform

The cloud platform is the focal point of the PhasmaFOOD system. Running on two virtual machines, it hosts the data warehouse, the rule engine for decision making, the web dashboard and the machine learning 'playground', a tool for configuring new machine learning pipelines for each available dataset. For each use case exists a labelled dataset in the data warehouse, on which machine learning algorithms for each sensor are trained. These datasets are produced by experts in food chemistry laboratories and contain measurements with additional instruments that give ground truth values for the quantities of interest that the PhasmaFOOD system attempts to predict, i.e. aflatoxin contamination for use case 1, microbia counts and age of the samples for use case 2 and information on adulterands for use case 3. Based on these decision making algorithms, the rule engine outputs a verdict on the food quality of an incoming measurement, which is presented to the user in the mobile app. Details on the cloud functionality can be found in [3].

3 Data analysis strategy

The different steps that transform the raw measurements into a food quality verdict are distributed across the PhasmaFOOD system. Simple preprocessing of the sensor data is done in the electronics subsystem of the PhasmaFOOD device, whereas the extraction of high level features and the final prediction is currently done on the cloud platform. A redistribution of these decision making steps to the mobile app or even the device to optimize the use of resources will be subject of further investigation in the last stage of the PhasmaFOOD project. The decision making is based on supervised learning methods. While simple preprocessing steps are the same for all food types under consideration, the computation of expressive features and the best prediction algorithm for a certain quantity of interest vary with use case and food type. Hence, for each labelled dataset corresponding to a use case and food type a variety of models are trained and evaluated to find a suitable analysis strategy. The data recorded with the spectrometers only amount to a few kilobytes. Thus, there is no need to perform compression on the embedded device. The image data on the other hand requires special treatment to reduce the traffic over the BLE connection from the device to the mobile app and subsequently to the cloud.

3.1 Structured dictionary learning

It is desirable to reduce the size of the images (ca. 15Mb) significantly thereby retaining the significant information for later classification. Since natural images are highly redundant, a common idea for lossy compression is to represent the image as a linear combination of suitably chosen dictionary atoms. General purpose lossy compression algorithms like JPEG or JPEG2000 use fixed dictionaries such as cosine atoms or wavelet atoms, respectively that are well suited to represent natural images. While these algorithms focus entirely on good reconstruction of all natural images, measured by human perception, the goal for image compression in the PhasmaFOOD project is different. Each use case and food type produces a very narrow class of images that look very similar, with subtle variations due to spoilage of aged or adulterated food samples. These variations must be captured for further analysis at the same time reducing the ammount of dat to be transfered. Finally, since the compression/feature extraction algorithm runs on the embedded device, it should be fast and with low computational complexity. Therefore, the idea is to learn a data-adapted dictionary that focusses on sparse and discriminative encoding. The time-consuming learning part can be done offline on the cloud platform. For the encoding with the learned dictionary fast algorithms exist that can be run on the device as shown in figure 3.1. Dictionary

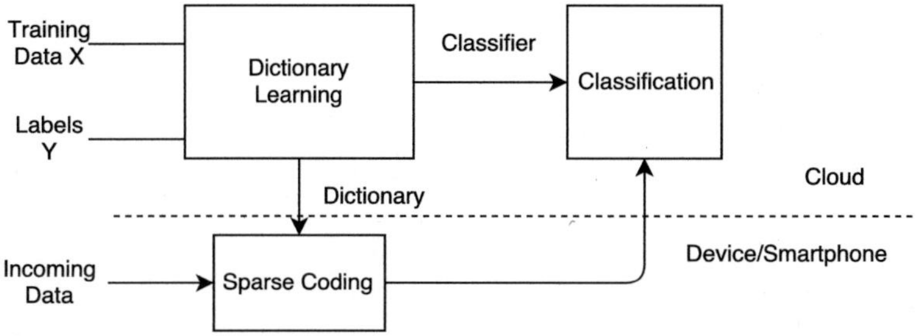

Figure 10.1: Compression scheme.

learning [4] has proven a successful technique for a variety of imaging task, such as sparse coding, denoising or image inpainting. In its basic form, it solves the problem

$$\min_{D,A} \|X - DA\|_2^2 + \lambda\|A\|_1 \quad \text{subject to } \|d_l\|_2 = 1 \quad \text{for } l = 0, 1, 2, \ldots, \tag{10.1}$$

where $D \in \mathbb{R}^{n\times N}$ is the dictionary to be learned, $X \in \mathbb{R}^{n\times m}$ is the matrix of training samples and $A \in \mathbb{R}^{N\times m}$ the matrix containing the codes. The regularization term $\lambda\|A\|_1$ enforces sparsity in the codes and the columns d_l of the dictionary are constrained to have unit norm to avoid scaling ambiguities. The problem can be solved by iteratively alternating between computing the codes A thereby keeping D fixed, i.e. sparse coding, and updating the dictionary atoms to better represent the data for fixed sparse codes. Additional terms can be incorporated in the objective function to induce task-specific properties of the solution. In [5] a classification loss was added to render the problem supervised, in [6] label information was included via a Fisher discrimination criterion. In [7] the dictionary was structured into a common and class-specific parts, which was used in [8] for fine-grained image classification. This approach is adopted here and combined with incoherence promoting terms [9] that stabilize the sparse coding and encourage the sub-dictionaries to encode different information. Let the dictionary be partitioned as $D = [D_0, D_1, \ldots, D_L]$, where $D_0 \in \mathbb{R}^{n\times N_0}$ is the common dictionary and $D_j \in \mathbb{R}^{n\times N_j}$ for $j = 1, \ldots, L$ are the class specific dictionaries. As another minor modification to the basic problem 10.1, instead of the l_1 regularization of A, here the number of nonzeros is constrained directly to be $\leq s$. Each sample x_i with corresponding label y_i is encoded only using D_0 and D_{y_i}. With the aforementioned incoherence terms the objective becomes

$$f(D, A) = \|X - DA\|_2^2 + \sum_{j=0}^{L} \mu_j \|D_j^T D_{-j}\|_2^2 + \sum_{j=0}^{L} \eta_j \|D_j^T D_j - I_{N_j}\|_2^2, \quad (10.2)$$

where D_{-j} denotes the dictionary composed of all but the jth sub-dictionary and I_N is the $N \times N$ identity matrix. Let $\mathcal{S}_j$ denote the indices of dictionary atoms belonging to the jth sub-dictionary. Then the discriminative encoding property of the codes can be expressed as the constraint

$$a_i\Big(\bigcup_{k \notin \{0,j\}} \mathcal{S}_k\Big) = 0 \text{ if } y_i = j. \quad (10.3)$$

The sparse coding step for a training sample x_i with label y_i takes the form

$$\min_a \|x_i - [D_0, D_{y_i}]a\|_2^2 \quad \text{subject to } |a|_0 \leq s, \quad (10.4)$$

which can be solved efficiently by orthogonal matching pursuit (OMP) [10]. OMP only needs to compute inner products between the sample and the dictionary atoms and is hence suited to run on the embedded device, which has only limited capacities.

For the dictionary update step the algorithm in [9] is employed. Denote by X_j the samples in class j and A_j the corresponding sparse codes. Set

$$Z_j = X_j - D_0 A_j(\mathcal{S}_0) \qquad \text{for } j = 1, \ldots, L,$$
$$Z_0 = X - [D_1, \ldots, D_L] A(\mathcal{S}_{-0}).$$

Computing the derivative of the objective with respect to a sub-dictionary D_j and setting the result to 0, $\frac{\partial f(D_j)}{\partial D_j} = 0$ leads to a Sylvester-type matrix equation

$$PD_j + D_j Q = R \quad (10.5)$$

with the matrices

$$P = \mu_j D_{-j} D{-j}^T,$$
$$Q = A_j(\mathcal{S}_j) A_j(\mathcal{S}_j)^T + \eta_j D_j^T D_j - I_{N_j},$$
$$R = Z_j A_j(\mathcal{S}_j)^T.$$

The Sylvester equation could be solved by the Bartels-Stewart algorithm [11], if Q and R were independent of D_j. Following [9], an approximate solution to equation 10.5 can be obtained by intializing $D_j^0 = D_j$ and then solving $PD_j + D_jQ^t = R^t$ for a few iterations, where Q^t and R^t are computed using D_j^{t-1} (normalized to have unit norm columns) and the updated sparse codes.

To apply the described algorithm the raw image is first scaled to the range $[0, 1]$ in each channel, then a square region of interest is extracted to exclude the edges of the sample holder. The selcted region is divided into non-overlapping patches of shape $(p \times p \times 3)$, which then serve as input to the algorithm, resulting in dictionary atom size $3p^2$. The sparse codes of an image's patches can be quantized and entropy coded to further reduce the size, if needed. In the cloud, an SVM is trained on the sparse codes of the training samples, resulting in a verdict for each image patch.

4 Discussion and conclusion

Although the literature on dictionary learning suggests good results in terms of compression rates and high accuracies have been achieved in classification tasks using structured dictionaries, the performance of the presented approach for the specific application in the context of PhasmaFOOD remains to be thoroughly investigated once enough labelled data has been collected. Furthermore, image data may not in all use cases contain information about the state of the food samples under consideration. This must be taken into account in data fusion strategies. In case one sensor does not contain useful information, a high level fusion strategy, i.e. combining the single predictions together to get a final verdict can simply assign a low weight to the useless sensor. In low level data fusion approaches this useless sensor might severly distort the classifier, unless a very strict feature selection method is used.

5 Summary

In this article the PhasmaFOOD system architecture was described. An approach to image compression and feature extraction based on learning a structured dictionary from labelled training data was presented in detail. The training of this dictionary is time consuming, but can be done offline on powerful computers, whereas the encoding of an image with it can be done on an embedded device efficiently by using OMP.

References

1. PhasmaFOOD, "Deliverable report d5.2: Hardware processing platform, storage and communication units integration -v1," 2018.
2. T. Pügner, J. Knobbe, H. Grüger, and H. Schenk, "Realization of a hybrid-integrated mems scanning grating spectrometer," in *Next-generation spectroscopic technologies V*, vol. 8374. International Society for Optics and Photonics, 2012, p. 83740W.
3. PhasmaFOOD, "Deliverable report d4.1: First implementation of software for phasmafood smart food analysis system," 2018.
4. M. Aharon, M. Elad, A. Bruckstein *et al.*, "K-svd: An algorithm for designing overcomplete dictionaries for sparse representation," *IEEE Transactions on signal processing*, vol. 54, no. 11, p. 4311, 2006.
5. J. Mairal, J. Ponce, G. Sapiro, A. Zisserman, and F. R. Bach, "Supervised dictionary learning," in *Advances in neural information processing systems*, 2009, pp. 1033–1040.
6. M. Yang, L. Zhang, X. Feng, and D. Zhang, "Sparse representation based fisher discrimination dictionary learning for image classification," *International Journal of Computer Vision*, vol. 109, no. 3, pp. 209–232, 2014.
7. S. Kong and D. Wang, "A dictionary learning approach for classification: separating the particularity and the commonality," in *European Conference on Computer Vision*. Springer, 2012, pp. 186–199.
8. S. Gao, I. W.-H. Tsang, and Y. Ma, "Learning category-specific dictionary and shared dictionary for fine-grained image categorization," *IEEE Transactions on Image Processing*, vol. 23, no. 2, pp. 623–634, 2014.

9. M. Nejati, S. Samavi, N. Karimi, S. M. R. Soroushmehr, and K. Najarian, "Boosted dictionary learning for image compression." *IEEE Trans. Image Processing*, vol. 25, no. 10, pp. 4900–4915, 2016.
10. J. A. Tropp and A. C. Gilbert, "Signal recovery from random measurements via orthogonal matching pursuit," *IEEE Transactions on information theory*, vol. 53, no. 12, pp. 4655–4666, 2007.
11. R. H. Bartels and G. W. Stewart, "Solution of the matrix equation ax + xb = c [f4]," *Commun. ACM*, vol. 15, no. 9, pp. 820–826, Sep. 1972.

Optical characterization with filter-on-chip CMOS sensor-systems

P.-G. Dittrich[1,2], L. Radtke[1], C. Zhang[1], S. Guo[1], B. Buch[1], M. Rosenberger[1], and G. Notni[1]

[1] Technische Universität Ilmenau,
Department of Mechanical Engineering,
Group for Quality Assurance and Industrial Image Processing,
Gustav-Kirchhoff-Platz 2, 98693 Ilmenau, Germany
[2] SpectroNet c/o Technologie- und Innovationspark Jena GmbH,
Hans-Knöll-Straße 6, 07745 Jena, Germany

Abstract Mosaic filter-on-chip CMOS sensors enable the parallel acquisition of spatial and spectral information. These mosaic sensors are characterized by spectral filters which are applied directly on the sensor pixel in a matrix which is multiplied in the x- and y-direction over the entire sensor surface. Current mosaic sensors for the visible wavelength range using 9 or 16 different spectral filters in 3×3 or 4×4 matrices. Methods for the reconstruction of spectral reflectance from multispectral resolving sensors have been developed. It is known that the spectral reflectance of most natural objects can be approximated with a limited number of spectral base functions. In these cases continuous spectral distributions can be reconstructed from multispectral data of a limited number of channels. This paper shows how continuous spectral distributions can be reconstructed using spectral reconstruction methods like Moore-Penrose pseudoinverse, Wiener estimation, Polynomial reconstruction and Reverse principal component analysis. These methods will be evaluated with monolithic mosaic sensors. The Goodness of Fit Coefficient and the CIE color difference are used to evaluate the reconstruction results.

Keywords: Multispectral, filter-on-chip, spectral reconstruction.

1 Introduction

To meet the growing expectations concerning the quality in industry, biology and medicine miniaturized photonic micro sensors are now available for simultaneous optical characterization of shapes, colors and spectra.

The latest developments in photonic micro sensor systems enable simultaneous recording of those information with specialized multispectral resolving mosaic filter-on-chip CMOS sensors.

2 Sensor technology

The mosaic filter-on-chip CMOS sensors are characterized by spectral filters which are applied directly on the sensor pixel in a matrix which is multiplied in the x- and y-direction over the entire active sensor surface. Current mosaic sensors for the visible wavelength range using 9 or 16 different spectral filters in 3×3 or 4×4 matrices.

For the realization of these sensors two technologies are used. First is a monolithic approach where the filters are directly applied on the CMOS sensor surface. Second is a hybrid approach where the filters are applied on a separate substrate and the substrate is afterwards arranged on the CMOS sensor surface [1].

3 Methods and algorithms

The following section provides a general guideline for the application of multispectral resolving mosaic filter-on-chip CMOS-sensor-systems in the visible wavelength range. This includes the performed metrological characterization of the system, the derived correction of the sensor data, the derived sensor value extension and the provision of ready to use sensor data for final application (Figure 11.1).

With the metrological characterization of the spectral, optical and electrical properties of the sensor-system a value correction and extension model can be derived [2], [3]. Using pre-characterized properties, a correction matrix for the pixel reflectance can be calculated to minimize spectral crosstalk [4], [5]. With the acquisition of dark and white

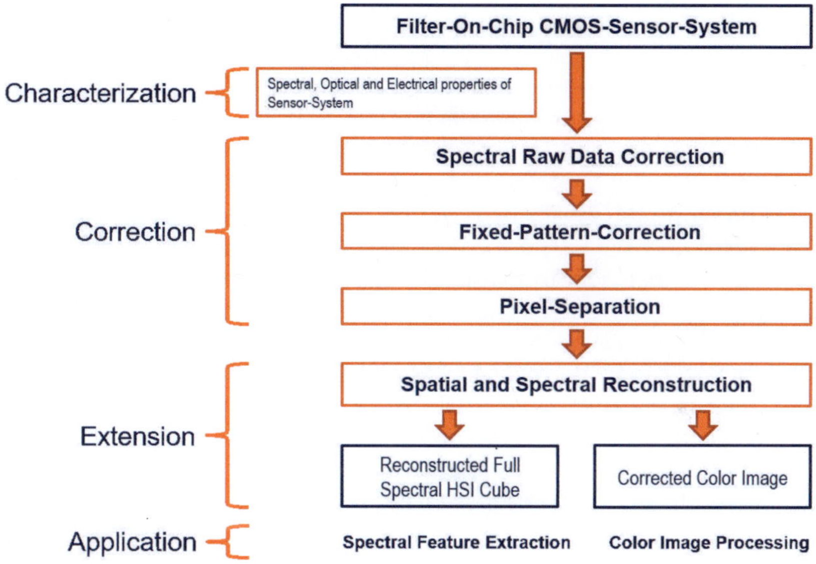

Figure 11.1: Characterization, correction and extension model for mosaic filter-on-chip CMOS-sensor-systems.

reference images during the pre-characterization a fixed pattern correction for the correction of intensity differences per spectral band can be implemented for the purpose of pixel value harmonization [6].

Afterwards a pixel separation for the alignment of the separated multispectral sub-images among themselves can be applied. Furthermore, shifts in the measured spectra can be minimized by a finite aperture correction [7]. For the sensor value extension typical reconstruction methods can be categorized into linear and nonlinear techniques.

Examples for linear techniques are Moore-Penrose pseudo-inverse (*MPPI*) [8], Wiener estimation (*Wiener*) [9] and Reverse principal component analysis (*PCA*) [10]. Nonlinear estimation methods like Polynomial reconstruction (*Poly*) [11] have more variations, but some of them can be considered as combinations of multiple linear estimations. Some of the reconstruction methods require an iterative process, such as the ones based on compressive sensing theory [12]. It is known that the spectral reflectance of most natural objects can be approximated with a limited number of spectral base functions. In these cases the continuous spectral distributions can be reconstructed from multispectral data of a limited number of channels [12].

The paper will show how continuous spectral distributions can be reconstructed using these reconstruction methods for monolithic mosaic filter-on-chip CMOS-sensor-systems. The Goodness of Fit Coefficient (*GFC*) [13] and the CIE color difference (*DeltaE*) [14] are used to evaluate the reconstruction results of experimental measurements with a 16-channel monolithic mosaic filter-on-chip CMOS camera.

For the accuracy of colorimetry, the *GFC* must be at least 0.995 [15]. $GFC > 0.999$ is to be regarded as a good fit and $GFC > 0.9999$ as a perfect fit of the spectra [14]. CIEDE2000 is a CIE recommended color difference formula that contains new terms for improving the predicted color difference in the blue range and for neutral colors for pairs of samples with small color differences [15].

4 Results and summary

In the following section the spectral reconstruction methods will be evaluated under realistic conditions. For every evaluation the following data is necessary: Spectral characteristics of the multispectral resolving sensor (Figure 11.2, left), target sets for calibration and reconstruction which consist of the reflectance spectra of different "Colorcheckers" (Figure 11.2, middle) and a radiation spectrum of an illuminant (Figure 11.2, right).

By pointwise multiplication of the spectral characteristics of the multispectral resolving sensor with the reflection spectra of the reconstruction set, the sensor-system responses are determined. Then the reconstruction matrices of Moore-Penrose pseudo-inverse, Wiener estimation, Reverse PCA and Polynomial reconstruction are calculated. In the investigation, the coupling factor p will be 0.99 for Wiener estimation and the number of principal components for PCA l will be 8. After the sensor-system responses are determined the reflection spectra are reconstructed using the reconstruction matrices. The standard light *D50* is assumed to be the recording light source when converting from spectrum to L*a*b* color space. Under the standard observer assumptions with 2° field of view, the color difference between the measured and reproduced colors were determined. At the end, the reconstructed spectra are evaluated according to *GFC*.

Furthermore the color differences in the visible wavelength range from 380 to 780 nm where analyzed. In the evaluation, the mean value, the minimum value and the median value of all reconstructed reflection spectra by *GFC* are named GFC_{Mean}, GFC_{Min} and GFC_{Median} respectively. The mean, minimum, and median of all color differences are named as $DeltaE_{Mean}$, $DeltaE_{Min}$, and $DeltaE_{Median}$.

For the practical evaluation the Colorchecker Passport is used as calibration set. The Spydercheker is used as the reconstruction set. The multispectral images are acquired with a digital resolution of 10 bits. To minimize random noise, 25 images of the calibration and reconstruction set were chosen and the mean value of the images was calculated for further processing. The reflectance spectra of the reconstruction set which are measured with a spectrometer are shown as Ground Truth to evaluate the performance of the reconstruction methods (Figure 11.3).

The reconstruction results of *MPPI*, *Wiener*, *Poly* and *PCA* were evaluated with GFC_{Mean}, GFC_{Min} and GFC_{Median} (Table 11.1).

The Poly reconstruction method shows the best approximation of the reconstructed spectra to the Ground Truth. Furthermore, the $DeltaE_{Mean}$ values of the reconstruction set were determined (Figure 11.4).

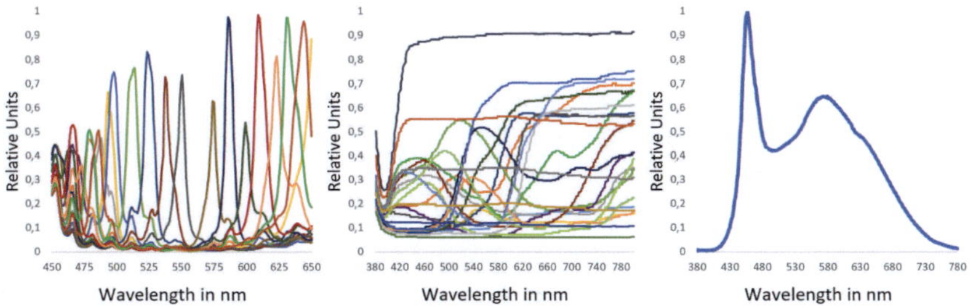

Figure 11.2: Example data for the evaluation of spectral reconstruction methods.

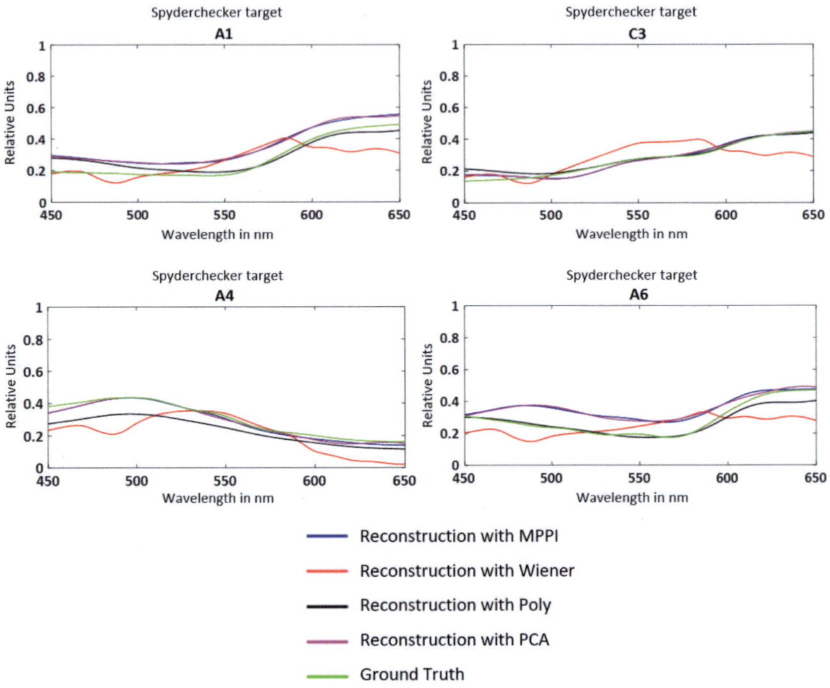

Figure 11.3: Evaluation of different reconstruction methods for 16-channel mosaic filter-on-chip CMOS camera (reconstructed spectra).

In the graph, the $DeltaE_{Mean}$ values according to spectral reconstruction methods are displayed for every color number of the Spyderchecker reconstruction set. Furthermore, the average of the $DeltaE_{Mean}$ values is displayed for the spectral reconstruction methods.

To illustrate the color deviation in the reconstructed color images the color differences determined for the targets of the reconstruction set are plotted on the respective target (Figure 11.5).

The color difference of the reproduced colors in *MPPI* and *PCA* can be easily perceived by human eyes. This is where the limited wavelength range of the camera becomes noticeable.

Table 11.1: Evaluation of different reconstruction methods for a monolithic mosaic sensor (GFC_{Mean}, GFC_{Min} and GFC_{Median}).

	GFC_{Mean}	GFC_{Min}	GFC_{Median}
MPPI	0.9949	0.9727	0.9981
Wiener	0.9594	0.9414	0.9594
Poly	**0.9986**	**0.9944**	**0.9990**
PCA	0.9947	0.9712	0.9976

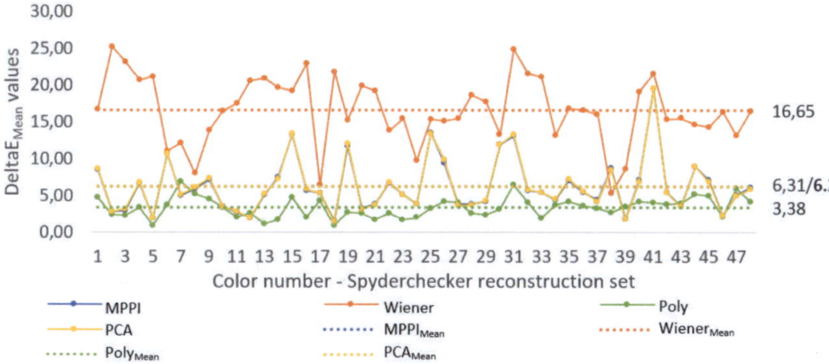

Figure 11.4: Evaluation of different reconstruction methods for a monolithic mosaic sensor ($DeltaE_{Mean}$, $DeltaE_{Min}$ and $DeltaE_{Median}$).

The paper gives an overview about the characterization and correction of mosaic filter-on-chip CMOS-sensor-systems. Furthermore, the paper shows how continuous spectral distributions can be reconstructed using a 16-channel monolithic mosaic filter-on-chip CMOS-sensor-system with spectral reconstruction methods. Methods for the evaluation of spectral reconstruction and color calculation have been shown. For the evaluation of spectral reconstruction methods with multispectral resolving filter-on-chip CMOS-sensor-systems a combination of target sets for calibration and reconstruction have been investigated. It could be shown that in the performed evaluation Polynominal reconstruction method provides the most robust and accurate approaches for the spectral reconstruction with multispectral resolving mosaic filter-on-chip CMOS-sensor-systems.

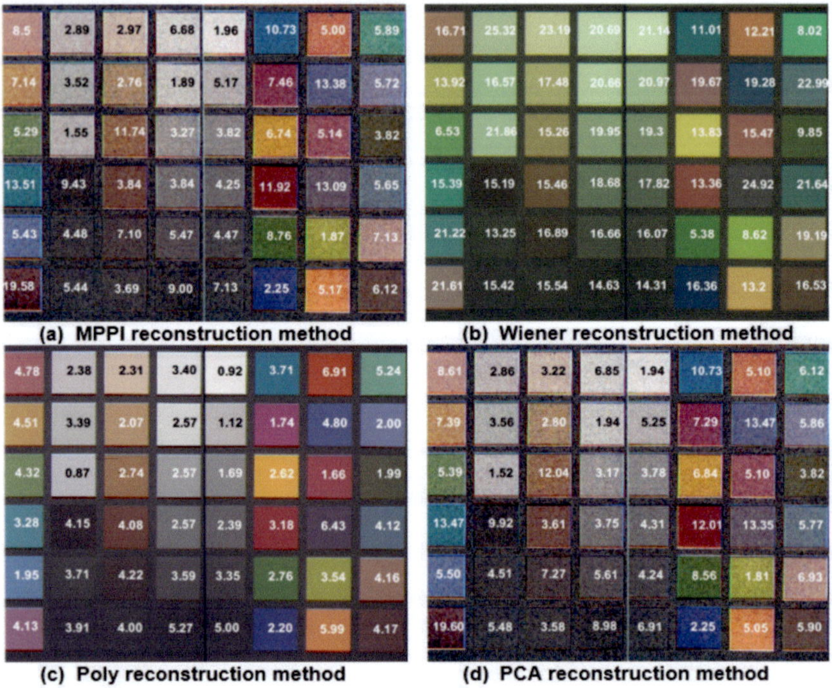

Figure 11.5: Evaluation of different reconstruction methods for 16-channel mosaic filter-on-chip CMOS camera (reconstructed color images and $DeltaE_{Mean}$ values).

It should be noted that the results have been evaluated in a lab environment. Current monolithic mosaic filter-on-chip CMOS cameras cannot cover the entire visible wavelength range for correct color calculation because of limitations in the filter technology and the usage of additional bandpass filters.

Multispectral resolving mosaic filter-on-chip CMOS cameras provide a new approach for Multi-/Hyperspectral Imaging. It has been shown that an extended sensor model can be developed and used to get corrected and extended sensor data for improving the capabilities of these cameras in optical characterization tasks.

References

1. S. Tisserand, "Multispektrale bildgebung mit angepassten bayer-filtern," 02 2017.
2. European Machine Vision Association, "Emva standard 1288 characterization of cameras," 2010.
3. J. Y. Hardeberg, B. H., and F. J. M. Schmitt, "Spectral characterization of electronic cameras," 1998.
4. J. Pichette *et al.*, "Hyperspectral calibration method for cmos-based hyperspectral sensors." 2017.
5. V. Sauget, M. Hubert, A. Faiola, and S. Tisserand, "Application note for cms camera & cms sensor users post-processing method for crosstalk reduction in multispectral data & images." 2017.
6. P. Schwider, "New hyperspectral cmos cameras and software development kits for universal applications," 2017.
7. T. Goossens, B. Geelen, J. Pichette, A. Lambrechts, and C. Van Hoof, "Finite aperture correction for spectral cameras with integrated thin-film fabry–perot filters," 2018.
8. A. Arthur, "Regression and the moore-penrose pseudoinverse," 1972.
9. W. K. Pratt and C. E. Mancill, "Spectral estimation techniques for the spectral calibration of a color image scanner," 1976.
10. P. Burns and R. S. Berns, "Analysis of multispectral image capture," 1996.
11. D. R. Connah and J. Y. Hardeberg, "Spectral recovery using polynomial models," 2005.
12. CIE Central Bureau, "Multispectral image formats," 2017.
13. J. Hernández-Andrés, J. Romero, and R. L. Lee, "Colorimetric and spectroradiometric characteristics of narrow-field-of-view clear skylight in granada, spain," 2001.
14. G. Sharma, W. Wu, and E. N. Dalal, "The ciede2000 color-difference formula: Implementation notes, supplementary test data, and mathematical observations," 2005.
15. C. Matasaru, "Mobile phone camera possibilities for spectral imaging," 2014.